TREKKING GRAN PARADISO:
ALTA VIA 2

FROM CHARDONNEY TO COURMAYEUR
IN THE AOSTA VALLEY

by Gillian Price

JUNIPER HOUSE, MURLEY MOSS,
OXENHOLME ROAD, KENDAL, CUMBRIA LA9 7RL
www.cicerone.co.uk

© Gillian Price 2024
First edition 2024
ISBN. 978 1 78631 184 9

Printed in Czechia on behalf of Latitude Press Ltd using responsibly sourced paper.
A catalogue record for this book is available from the British Library.
Maps by Nicola Regine
All photographs are by the author unless otherwise stated.

Dedication

To dear Nicola with all my love

Acknowledgements

I would like to acknowledge the majestic ibex, shy chamois and comical marmots, too numerous to name individually, who make this area so special.

Updates to this guide

While every effort is made by our authors to ensure the accuracy of guidebooks as they go to print, changes can occur during the lifetime of an edition. Any updates that we know of for this guide will be on the Cicerone website (www.cicerone.co.uk/1184/updates), so please check before planning your trip. We also advise that you check information about such things as transport, accommodation and shops locally. Even rights of way can be altered over time. We are always grateful for information about any discrepancies between a guidebook and the facts on the ground, sent by email to updates@cicerone.co.uk or by post to Cicerone, Juniper House, Murley Moss, Oxenholme Road, Kendal LA9 7RL.

    Register your book: To sign up to receive free updates, special offers and GPX files where available, create a Cicerone account and register your purchase via the 'My Account' tab at www.cicerone.co.uk.

Front cover: Comba des Usselettes on the way to Rifugio Deffeyes (Stage 10)

CONTENTS

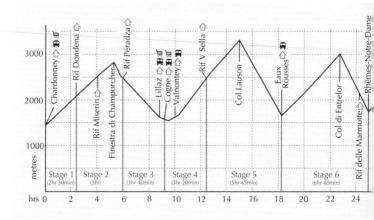

It's a long but easy walk up Vallone de Chavannes (Stage 11)

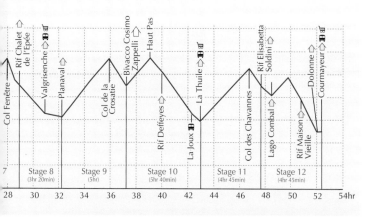

Col Fenêtre
Rif Chalet de l'Epée ⬆
Valgrisenche ⬆
Planaval ⬆
Col de la Crosatie
Bivacco Cosimo Zappelli ⬆
Haut Pas
Rif Deffeyes ⬆
La Joux
La Thuile ⬆
Col des Chavannes
Rif Elisabetta Soldini ⬆
Lago Combal ⬆
Rif Maison Vieille
Dolonne ⬆
Courmayeur ⬆

7	Stage 8 (3hr 20min)	Stage 9 (5hr)	Stage 10 (5hr 40min)	Stage 11 (4hr 45min)	Stage 12 (4hr 45min)	
28	30 32	34 36	38 40 42	44 46	48 50 52	54hr

Mountain safety

Every mountain walk has its dangers, and those described in this guidebook are no exception. All who walk or climb in the mountains should recognise this and take responsibility for themselves and their companions along the way. The author and publisher have made every effort to ensure that the information contained in this guide was correct when it went to press, but, except for any liability that cannot be excluded by law, they cannot accept responsibility for any loss, injury or inconvenience sustained by any person using this book.

International distress signal *(emergency only)*
Six blasts on a whistle (and flashes with a torch after dark) spaced evenly for one minute, followed by a minute's pause. Repeat until an answer is received. The response is three signals per minute followed by a minute's pause.

Helicopter rescue
The following signals are used to communicate with a helicopter:

Help needed:
raise both arms
above head to
form a 'Y'

Help not needed:
raise one arm
above head, extend
other arm downward

Emergency telephone numbers
General emergency tel 112
Soccorso alpino (mountain rescue) tel 118

Weather reports
https://cf.regione.vda.it/

Mountain rescue can be very expensive – be adequately insured.

ROUTE SUMMARY TABLE

Stage	Time	Distance	Ascent/Descent	Grade	Page
1	2hr 30min	5.8km	750m/–	1–2	32
2	3hr	7.8km	650m/300m	2	34
3	3hr 40min	15km	100m/1100m	2	38
4	3hr 20min	8.5km	1050m/–	1–2	41
5	5hr 45min	16.5km	750m/1650m	2–3	44
6	6hr 40min	16km	1350m/1300m	2	63
7	4hr	7.4km	1150m/500m	2–3	67
8	3hr 20min	13.5km	50m/900m	1–2	70
9	5hr	10km	1400m/700m	2–3	73
10	5hr 40min	14km	700m/1500m	2	76
11	4hr 45min	18km	1200m/490m	2	80
12	4hr 45min	15km	500m/1500m	2	83
Totals	**52hr 25min**	**147.5km**	**9650m/9940m**		
Extension route (skipping Stages 6 and 7):					
Stage A	4hr 40min	10.5km	1010m/450m	2	49
Stage B	4hr	10km	650m/900m	2–3	53
Stage C	5hr (+1hr optional summit)	10km	850m/860m	2–3	56
Stage D	4hr 15min	17km	310m/1035m	1–2	60

Comba des Usselettes and Rifugio Deffeyes (Stage 10)

INTRODUCTION

Located in northwest Italy, straddling the Piemonte and the Valle d'Aosta regions, the Gran Paradiso National Park is synonymous with majestic soaring mountains and rugged valleys home to fascinating wildlife.

The ibex is the symbol of the Parco Nazionale Gran Paradiso

'Intending visitors to the district should be warned that when the King of Italy is hunting around Cogne (the present King has not been there since 1885) they may find their movements impeded by fear of disturbing the game. This will seem however but a small hindrance when set against the great facilities which the royal hunting paths (passable for horses) afford to travellers on the less interesting portions of many of the ascents in this group.'

This introduction appeared in 1893 in *The Mountains of Cogne* (by George Yeld and Reverend WAB Coolidge), one of the first guides to the area to be published. Hunting was prohibited back in 1821 – except by royal entourages – ostensibly to protect the ibex and chamois populations, which were at worryingly low levels. Then in 1856 King Vittorio Emanuele II declared the area a Royal Game Reserve. Five hunting lodges were constructed along with 350km of tracks, all manned by a veritable army of gamekeepers (otherwise known as converted poachers), beaters and porters. In 1922 Vittorio Emanuele III renounced his hunting rights and declared Italy's very first national park 'for the purpose of protecting the fauna and flora, and preserving the special geological formations, as well as the beauty of the scenery'. Nowadays it encompasses 70,000 hectares (700km²) with 470km of marked paths linking alpine meadows below magnificent mountains and glaciers, wild valleys and traditional hamlets. A group of 50 rangers monitor wildlife.

Trekkers will enjoy unforgettable days on excellent trails through spectacular valleys that they have all to themselves, even at the height of the summer season.

GRAN PARADISO

An ibex at rest below the Gran Paradiso mountain

The romantic name Gran Paradiso goes back much further than the kings. The national park took its name from the 4061m mountain (the only 4000+m summit wholly in Italy), whose name derives either from *granta parei* ('great wall'), if not from the host of saintly peaks at the head of Valnontey – San Pietro, San Andrea and Sant'Orso, which counteract neighbouring Punta dell'Inferno and Testa della Tribolazione!

In geological terms, the Gran Paradiso summit is a huge dome of augengneiss girdled by calcareous rock, mica schists and greenstone.

The first recorded ascent dates back to 1860, by English climbers JJ Cowell and W Dundas with French guides Michel Payot and Jean Tairraz. As they weren't equipped with crampons, they had to cut over 1000 steps in the ice. The ascent did not immediately become popular so to encourage visitors in 1931 the mountaineer-priest Abbé Henry took a donkey called Cagliostro to the summit, fitting his hoofs with iron nails: 'If donkeys can go up the Gran Paradiso, then so can people...'.

ALTA VIA 2

Starting out on the eastern edge of the Gran Paradiso National Park, the exhilarating 147.5km, 12-day Alta Via 2 connects little-known Chardonney in Valle di Champorcher with the world-famous resort of Courmayeur, the gateway to Mont Blanc. It spells 12 memorable, energy-packed days on a roller-coaster walk dipping in and out of Vallon di Cogne, Valsavarenche and Val di Rhêmes, then on to Valgrisenche, Valle de la Thuile and Val Vény. Magnificent peaks dot the way – standouts include the Grivola, Herbetet and Ruitor, along with the massive Gran Paradiso. Europe's sovereign Mont Blanc – Monte Bianco to the Italians – provides the trek's breathtaking finale.

Marked by a black and yellow triangle and the number '2', the long-distance AV2 cuts its strenuous way across the rugged southern flanks of the Valle d'Aosta, over a sequence of forbidding crests and dizzy cols, worlds away from the busy traffic artery of the main valley. An excellent network of manned mountain huts (rifugi), hostels and modest inns welcome walkers and provide tasty hot meals and comfortable sleeping quarters.

Alta Via 2 waymarks

As if the AV2 needed any more to recommend it, the route is relatively untrodden, making for sublime solitary days after which all effort is amply rewarded with memorable traditional meals in well-run mountain huts and cosy village guesthouses. Picnic supplies can be replenished at shops on a fairly regular basis – and walkers can join and leave the route at will thanks to valley bus services.

On the whole the going is straightforward, suitable for average walkers with some alpine experience, although there is the odd stretch of unusually steep or exposed terrain.

An original four-day extension is also described to enable trekkers to admire the magnificent Gran Paradiso itself from closer quarters, then explore the upper reaches of Valsavarenche, Val di Rhêmes and Valgrisenche.

Naturally you can walk the AV2 in reverse, although that would mean – alas! – missing the thrill of the Mont Blanc conclusion. Approximate timing for walking in the opposite direction is given in the information box for each stage.

WILDLIFE

One of the reasons for visiting Gran Paradiso National Park is the marvellous opportunity for observing wildlife at close quarters. To state the obvious, the best way to spot animals is simply to look for them – most

Chamois at pasture

are masters of disguise and perfectly camouflaged in their natural habitat. Desolate rock-strewn cirques often reveal fawn patches which on closer inspection turn out to be chamois. Grassy terrain is pitted with holes leading to marmot burrows, while abandoned farm buildings overgrown with nettles double as homes to reptiles. Uninviting rock crests are worth perusing with binoculars for ibex sentinels – more often than not tracking the progress of walkers!

The elegant ibex, *Capra ibex*, is the undisputed king of the Gran Paradiso and the star of the park. Also known as bouquetin or steinbock, this stocky wild goat has enormous backward-curving ribbed horns, which grow to almost one metre on males, half for females. Males average 95 to 100kg, females around 65 to 70kg.

Well established and protected these days, they number a record 4000, in contrast to the 600 reported in 1860 and the 400 post-WW2 survivors. The original Gran Paradiso stock successfully repopulated the whole of alpine Europe.

Of a summer's evening, young males clash horns in mock battle in preparation for the December mating season. (Then it is anything but pretend with the females only on heat for 24 hours.) Sedate older males graze unperturbed, some distance from herds of timid females with their young.

Hunted intensely since medieval times, ibex were considered 'walking pharmacies' as their blood, horns, bones and even droppings were used to remedy everything from poisoning to rheumatism. A special talisman fashioned from the tiny cross-shaped bone found in the heart was believed to guard the wearer against a violent death.

Fleet-footed chamois, *Rupicapra rupicapra*, abound – a recent count recorded 7700 in the park. Slender and daintier, they sport short hooked horns, pale fawn coats and white patches on face and rear. Their principal predators are foxes and eagles but long snowy winters take a big toll on both the ibex and the chamois populations. Curiously, neither lose their horns, in contrast to the red and roe deer which inhabit lower wooded slopes.

It is hard to miss hearing the European alpine marmot (*Marmota marmota*) with its shrill whistle warning of imminent danger or seeing a well-padded rear scampering over grassy hillocks towards its burrow. These comical beaver-like vegetarians live in large underground colonies and 8000–10,000 were counted

A baby marmot

recently. Now protected, they were once hunted for their fat, which was used in ointments and believed to cure rheumatism. However, the belief was unfounded as it arose from a linguistic misunderstanding: the real 'marmot oil' for treating aches and pains comes from the Briançon apricot, otherwise known as the 'marmot plum'.

Red foxes are easily seen outside refuges at nightfall when they come to scavenge titbits from the rubbish. Much more difficult to spot is the elegant wolf (*Canis lupus*). Originally from the central Italian Apennines, they have stealthily spread across the Alps with two established packs here in the national park. The rangers say the park is the personal supermarket of the wolves and in return they help keep the hoofed animal population in check.

Another sizeable carnivore returning gradually westward across the Alps is the lynx. Sightings of the tufted-ear feline with grey-brown mottled fur have been reported in Valle d'Aosta, where it prefers the shelter of low altitude woods, the habitat of its favourite prey, the roe deer. (It is also known to hunt old ibex who are slower on their feet.)

In terms of amphibians, the common frog is renowned for its ability to spend winters frozen into lakes as high as 2500m, where temperatures can drop as low as −45°C! The resilient creatures thaw back to life with the arrival of spring. On dry southern

Early morning view from Rifugio Sella northeast (Stages 4–5)

hillsides the bright emerald sheen of the green lizard is hard to miss, while snakes sun themselves on paths or old stone walls. The most common is the poisonous (and protected) adder, otherwise known as a viper. This greyish-brown snake has a clear diamond head and zigzag pattern along its back. Extremely timid, it only attacks when threatened so do give it time to slither away. In the unlikely circumstance that someone is bitten, keep calm, stay put and seek medical help as quickly as possible. Bandaging of the bite area is usually recommended in the meantime.

Higher up, ubiquitous flocks of chaotic noisy orange-beaked crows, more correctly known as alpine choughs, glide. Great chatty socialisers, they appear out of nowhere at strategic cols at the rustling of a food wrapper, safe in the knowledge that they will be fed by walkers' crumbs. Their noise is only equalled by raucous European jays, which flash blue feathers on their dashes through the mixed woodlands lower down. Then there's the voracious Nutcracker. Easily spotted perching on tree tops, the industrious dappled crow-like bird is an expert at cracking pine cones with its thick beak. It is responsible for the survival of the Arolla pine as it hoards its kernels in rock crannies then forgets where 20% of them are hidden, so the trees sprout and grow in the most unlikely spots.

Impressive shadows are cast by majestic golden eagles (27 pairs call the park home), who have a field day in summer preying on young marmots, not to mention chamois and ibex. Amazingly, a 7kg eagle can fly off with prey weighing up to 20kg!

The eagles' only competition in terms of territory comes from the largest bird in the Alps, the lammergeier or bearded vulture. Slighter larger than the eagle and with an orange neck ruff, it boasts a three-metre wing span. Its wedge-shaped tail helps to distinguish it from the round tail of the eagle. A scavenger rather than a hunter, the lammergeier prefers feeding on carcasses. It is able to swallow bones up to 30cm in length (digestion then requiring 24 hours!) and cracks bones by dropping them from a great height to get to the marrow. The reintroduction of vultures born in captivity took off in 1986 in Austria and 1994 saw the first release in Italy. Sightings are now frequent as the park boasts three couples. An impressive stuffed specimen is on display at the Chavaney (Val di Rhêmes) Park Visitor Centre.

Other treats are the brilliant clouds of butterflies which vie with each other for brightness – notably the metallic hues of the common blue Icarus butterflies which flutter up from their puddles as walkers pass by. The rare red apollo perches on thistles, pale grey-cream but with trademark black and red 'eyes' on its wings, in the company of another beauty, the red and black burnet moth.

Last but not least is the so-called glacier flea, large numbers of which form widespread dark patches on the surface of glaciers and snow fields up to 3800m. It is one to two millimetres long, hairy or scaly, mottled brown and feeds on organic matter such as pollen carried by the wind. Red-tinted snow on the other hand may either mean cold-loving algae with a blood-red colouring, or sand from a far-off desert, incredible though it may seem.

PLANTS AND FLOWERS

An excellent place to admire the remarkable array of alpine plants is the Giardino Botanico Alpino 'Paradisia' in Valnontey, established in 1955 and named for the St Bruno lily *Paradisia liliastrum*. Over summer 1000 labelled alpine species flourish there and of these a good 250 are found wild in the park.

The woods are mainly mixed conifer, dominated by larch and Arolla pine, along with juniper shrubs. This habitat is shared with pretty pink alpenrose shrubs as well as wine-red martagon lilies and the minute creamy flowers of bilberry and cowberry, which are followed by their late-summer fruit. Curious dwarf versions of trees such as the net-leaved willow and ice-age relict dwarf birch are common.

The record holder for growing at altitude is glacier crowfoot, which grows up to 4200m. Also found high up are colonisers of screes and bare

Clockwise from top left: *Glacier crowfoot is an altitude record holder; edelweiss; purple orchid; fluffy cotton grass thrives on marshy ground; marvellous yellow gentian*

rock, such as lilac round-leaved pennycress and succulent saxifrage (rock breaker), which penetrate cracks. Further down, stunning carpets of white ranunculus and pasque flowers smother upper pasture basins such as the Piano del Nivolet. Marshland is often punctuated with soft white cotton grass and tiny carnivorous butterworts – the blue-violet common variety or yellow-white alpine type. The famous edelweiss is relatively unusual due to a lack of the calcareous terrain it prefers, but another ice-age relict, the rare twinflower, a delicate pink-white drooping bloom that grows on moss cushions on open grassland, can often be found. Elegant orchids are widespread in meadows; the dark reddish-brown black vanilla variety has a surprisingly strong cocoa aroma.

The alpine environment is extremely hostile to life in general and the growth and reproduction season for high-altitude vegetation can be as short as 60–70 days. Each species has developed survival techniques, ranging from thick hairy layers as protection from cold winds and evaporation (edelweiss), antifreeze in its leaves (glacier crowfoot), as well as ground-hugging forms that minimise exposure, allow the plant to exploit the heat from the earth and ensure protective snow cover (cushions of rock jasmine). In addition to the beating they get from the elements, many also risk being nibbled by chamois (who have a weakness for sugary large-flowered leopard's-bane) and marmots (who go for forget-me-nots) and even picked by humans.

To end on a 'spiritual' note, a quick mention of the insignificant-looking but strongly aromatic yellow genipi is in order. Found on stony grassland, it is both rare and protected, although local residents are allowed to gather a limited amount to prepare their beloved Genepì spirit – a perfect after-dinner drink with guaranteed digestive properties to boot.

A recommended rucksack companion for flower lovers is the Cicerone pocket guide *Alpine Flowers* (2019), while Grey-Wilson and Blamey's *Alpine Flowers of Britain and Europe* (Harper Collins, 1995) is the perfect reference book at home.

HOW TO GET THERE

The Alta Via 2 trek begins at Chardonney, a village in the park's southern reaches. There are numerous ways to get there (see below); they all conclude with a year-round local VITA bus from Hône-Bard up Valle di Champorcher to Chardonney. From Hône-Bard railway station (note that only slow regional trains stop there) cross to the western side of the train line and motorway and walk up to the nearby square of Hône and the bus stop. (The bus route actually starts at Verres 7km north, handier as all trains stop there).

By plane to Torino then train

The most convenient airport is Torino's Caselle www.aeroportoditorino.it, well served from the UK and European countries. The occasional coach goes direct to Aosta (www.transfervallee. eu/en/), otherwise local trains and buses convey passengers to the city centre and the main railway stations Torino Porta Nuova and Torino Porta Susa for ongoing services.

By plane to Milano then train

Milano is handy with two airports www.sea-aeroportimilano.it well served by UK, European and international companies. Both Malpensa and Linate have direct trains to Milano Centrale station for ongoing links via Chivasso to the Valle d'Aosta.

By car

Drivers have a good choice of spectacular itineraries: from France via the Mont Blanc tunnel or the Piccolo San Bernardo pass; or from Switzerland via the Gran San Bernardo pass and tunnel. From the south, as well as main SS26, the A5 autostrada (motorway) leads to Aosta and Courmayeur.

Local transport

For train information, ticket purchase and bookings go to www.trenitalia. com (tel 892021). If you buy an open ticket at a ticket office remember to stamp it in a machine at the platform before you travel; failure to do so can result in a fine.

Timetables for all bus services in the Valle d'Aosta are available at www. regione.vda.it/trasporti, and local tourist offices can also provide timetables. In Aosta, you can get information at the central bus station (_autostazione_) (tel 0165 262027) right across the road from the railway station.

When reading timetables or asking for information, you will need to know that _giornaliero_ (abbreviated as GG) means daily, _scolastico_ means during school term, _feriale_ means Monday to Saturday, and _festivo_ means Sunday or public holidays. _Sciopero_ means strike.

Services are very reasonably priced. Summer timetables take effect around mid June, ending early in September, depending on school term dates.

Bus companies and services:

*   Arriva (https://aosta.arriva.it) has a direct Milano-Aosta bus. They also serve the main valley including Aosta and Courmayeur, as well as the valleys La Thuile, Val di Rhêmes, Valgrisenche and Valsavarenche
*   FLIXBUS (www.flixbus.it) runs to Aosta from many northern Italian cities such as Milano and Torinos and several airports
*   SADEM (tel 035 289000, www. sadem.it) does Torino–Aosta bus

runs as well as serving Torino's Caselle airport

- SVAP (www.svap.it) serves the valleys of Cogne
- For info on the free Cogne shuttle bus (to Valnontey, Lillaz and Gimillan) contact the Cogne Tourist Office (www. cogneturismo.it, tel 0165 74040)
- VITA (www.vitagroup.it) serves Valle di Champorcher
- Trekbus, an on-demand minibus, links the Gran Paradiso valleys (Cogne, Valsavarenche, Val di Rhêmes and Valgrisenche) July–mid September if there is no public bus handy. For

bookings, tel 331 8688621 or 339 5443364 or email info@ cm-grandparadis.vda.it.

Getting home

From the trek finish at Courmayeur take a coach either through the tunnel to Chamonix in France or down to Aosta for a train. Otherwise, catch a long-distance bus to Milano or Torino.

WHEN TO GO

The park area and surrounds are open all year. The most suitable period for AV2 trekkers is when the winter snow recedes and the high-altitude refuges

The steep descent from Col Rosset (Extension Stage B)

operate, namely late June to late September.

For flower lovers, July is probably the best month. August is peak holiday time for Italians and valley accommodation best booked in advance. September and October bring crystal clear days, burnt autumn colours and deserted paths. Italy stays on summer time until late October, meaning a bonus of extra daylight for visitors. The choice is yours.

SHORTER AND LONGER ITINERARIES

The Alta Via 2, with its 12 stages, fits snugly into a two-week holiday. However a number of shorter and longer variants are worth taking into consideration if you have less – or more – time.

Three days

Short and sweet yet strenuous, this mini trek traverses the heart of the park from Cogne to Rhêmes-Notre-Dame. Catch the bus from Aosta to Cogne and follow directions for Stage 4 via Valnontey and up to Rifugio Vittorio Sella. The following spectacular day (as per Stage 5) heads over the AV2's highest pass, 3299m Col Lauson, before plunging to Eaux Rousses in Valsavarenche. Then comes a beautiful solitary traverse (Stage 6) over to Rhêmes-Notre-Dame where you can catch a bus back to Aosta, well satisfied.

Six days

Perfect for a week's holiday, the opening six stages of the AV2 are both superb and rewarding. You begin at Chardonney and finish several magnificent valleys and a clutch of breathtaking passes later at the village of Rhêmes-Notre-Dame where a bus takes you down to Aosta and its train connections. Naturally the remaining six days (Stages 7–12) on to the foot of Mont Blanc and Courmayeur are another plausible option – likewise highly recommended and easily accessed using public transport.

A 14-day trek

Should you have a total of 14 days available (or be a fairly fit and fast walker), you may be interested in adding the two optional opening stages. Start out at Donnas – at a mere 330m altitude on the main Valle d'Aosta floor. A climb ensues via the hamlet of Crest (overnight stay at the dortoir, open May to Oct, tel 328 0514516, crestristorante@hotmail.com. Meals at the local restaurant a short walk away unless you self cater) then further on you join the main route at Chardonney. For details see https://www.lovevda.it/en/sport/trekking/alte-vie-trails/alta_via_2.

Extension

Last but not least, with a couple of extra days to spare, this original unofficial four-day extension to the AV2 is highly recommended. While it

Rifugio Sella in its marvellous setting (Stage 4)

skips Stages 6 and 7, it explores the spectacular southernmost realms of Valsavarenche, Val di Rhêmes and Valgrisenche. You leave the official route at the end of Stage 5 to visit Col del Nivolet, before climbing to Col Rosset then Rifugio Benevolo, followed by a traverse via Col Bassac Déré to Rifugio Bezzi and down to Valgrisenche, where you resume the AV2 at Stage 8. The extension route description with Stages A–D can be found after Stage 5.

ACCOMMODATION

Overnight stays on the 12 stages of the AV2 are split almost equally between high altitude mountain huts and valley accommodation so that should keep everyone happy. Only one day – Stage 9 – concludes at a modern

albeit unmanned hut though fit walkers can always push on.

All contact and practical details for accommodation can be found in the relevant stage, while Appendix A lists useful tourist offices where more options can be found.

Carry a good supply of euros in cash as credit cards are not accepted everywhere. Several villages and towns have ATMs – these are listed en route.

Wherever you stay, do settle your bill in the evening so as not to waste valuable time in the morning.

Rifugi

A stay in a refuge (*rifugio*; pl. *rifugi*) is a memorable part of the trek. These manned mountain huts include a converted hunting lodge, a former electricity board building, an old farm and a modern purpose-built building, all inevitably in scenic

ALPINE CLUBS

Membership of CAI is open to all nationalities. Intending members should apply to individual branches: the complete list can be found at www.cai. it. The annual fee is around €50 with half price rates for family members and 18–25 year olds, and less for children. As well as reductions in the huts across the Alps, this covers alpine rescue.

Brits can join the UK branch of the Austrian Alpine Club (www.alpen-verein.at/britannia). For North Americans there's the Canadian club www.alpineclubofcanada.ca and the US organisation https://americanalpineclub.org.

spots well away from roads. They provide drinks, snacks, meals and overnight accommodation throughout the summer months. The majority are run by the Italian Alpine Club (CAI, Club Alpino Italiano) as well as local families and alpine guides, and everyone is welcome. The staff share tasks ranging from cleaning, cooking, chopping wood, unloading supplies brought in by helicopter, cableway, horseback and backpack, greeting guests in different languages and dealing with emergencies.

As far as visitor facilities go, dormitories have bunk beds complete with pillows, blankets or a continental quilt, and there are occasionally smaller rooms with fresh linen for a bit more privacy. A lightweight personal sleeping sheet is needed in CAI huts and recommended elsewhere. Bathrooms are shared and fitted out with washbasins, mirrors and toilet cubicles – loo paper is always provided. Take your own towel. Assume all huts provide a *doccia calda* (hot shower) unless mentioned otherwise.

You may need to ask for a *gettone* (token) to operate the shower and be warned that water flow is limited.

By all means rinse out your day's gear and hang it outside but remember to get it in at night as otherwise it will be soaked by dew!

'Lights out' is 10pm–6am when the generator is usually turned off. Walking boots need to be left on racks in the hallway; slippers are sometimes provided. In line with Italian law, smoking is not allowed inside anywhere.

Mezza pensione or half board (meaning dinner, bed and breakfast) is common and usually an excellent deal. Charges are currently about €50–60 a night, not including drinks, or around €20 for a bed.

Generally speaking the summer opening period is mid June to late September. Exact dates vary year to year depending on holidays and local conditions, so if in doubt do check with the refuge beforehand, especially at the start or close of the season. Advance bookings are generally only necessary on July and August weekends. Should you change your mind, do notify the refuge to free up the bed and avoid expensive rescue operations (billed to you) being set in motion when you don't show up. Guests should sign the register and indicate their next destination as it could help point rescuers in the right direction in a search.

All refuges have a phone. To call from abroad use the Italian country code +39 and include the initial '0' when calling a landline. Mobile phones start with '3'.

Guesthouses

An *albergo* is a hotel, *locanda* and *pensione* mean guesthouse, while *affittacamere* is a B&B. Comfortable medium range options are given where useful in the route description. Others can be located through local tourist offices.

Bivouac huts

Unlike refuges, these are unmanned structures that are always open, free of charge and unbookable. They can be lifesavers in bad weather and users should ensure they leave the premises in good condition and close windows and doors properly. There is a single bivouac hut on the AV2, comfortable and modern, an essential overnight stop.

Walkers will also come across a series of modest huts, marked on maps as *Capanna* or *Casotto* PNGP.

They are used by the park rangers and are not available to walkers.

Camping

Wild camping is strictly forbidden in the Gran Paradiso National Park. It is allowed outside its borders but only above 2500m altitude from dusk to dawn. However, there are camping grounds in many valleys, several with bungalows. With a little juggling it is possible to plan on sleeping in a tent for approximately half of the AV2's 12 stages.

FOOD AND DRINK

Regional culinary specialities feature in meals in refuges and restaurants alike, a delight for gourmet visitors.

Meals begin with first course, a choice of classic Italian pasta dishes with sauces such as *ragù* or *pomodoro* (tomato). However soups are high on the menu. As well as the classic minestrone (with vegetables)

Valpellinentze soup

there's delicious Valpellinentenze with cabbage, fontina cheese and brown bread. *Seupetta di Cogne* on the other hand is a filling plate of rice with softened fontina and butter, cinnamon and croutons. Then there's risotto alla valdostana.

Next come second courses of meat and side dishes (*contorno*). One filling option is *polenta concia*, a scrumptious thick cornmeal porridge layered with melted butter and local cheese, or delicate *carbonada*, meat stewed in red wine with juniper berries. *Tartiflette* is a hearty fry-up of potatoes, onion, lard or pancetta and cheese irrigated with wine.

The Valle d'Aosta cheeses rate a chapter all of their own. Myriad and memorable, they are crafted on small farms which means no two have the same flavour. Using goat, cow and sheep's milk, they range from delicate and creamy through to mature, strong tasting and strikingly pungent. *Toma* refers to a smallish round of cheese, cow more often than not, from a local dairy. *Fontina*, the classic cheese

A mouth-watering choice of cheeses

for melting, comes in huge rounds. *Sargnun*, a tasty ricotta-like cheese comes fresh, salted or smoked, and is consumed with rye bread (*pane nero*), It used to be baked only twice a year, and was eaten rock hard, leading to the invention of those wooden bread boards with a built-in chopper that you will see on display.

Dessert will hopefully be creamy chocolatey custard *zuppa* or *crema di Cogne*, served with ultra-thin crunchy *tegole* biscuits.

Vegetarians, vegans and celiacs are well catered for – but do mention special dietary requirements when advance booking at refuges.

An excellent array of quality red and white wines come from the Valle d'Aosta vineyards. Don't miss a chance to try them – you won't be disappointed. These are supplemented by fuller-bodied Piemonte wines such as Barbera and Nebbiolo.

Stronger stuff comes in the form of aromatic *genepì*, known for its digestive properties and made from the flowers of the same name (not to be confused with juniper). It is served in miniature glasses, as is *grappa* (spirit), and flavoured with aromatic herbs or fruit. The *grolla*, a decorated covered wooden bowl with multiple mouth-pieces, may appear after dinner – filled with a memorable mixture of coffee, red wine, grappa, sugar and lemon. It is passed around for measured sips and so called the 'cup of friendship'.

WHAT TO TAKE

The choice of gear for a trekking holiday is crucial. It is worth spending time beforehand on careful preparation. Gear to cover all weather extremes is essential but be strict with yourself and remember you'll be carrying your stuff over the mountains day after day. Safety is paramount: an over-heavy rucksack can put walkers off balance and lead to falls and accidents.

The following checklist should help:

- Comfortable lightweight rucksack (25-litre capacity should do) with waist straps
- Walking boots with ankle support and non-slip Vibram-type soles, preferably not brand new. Trail running shoes are also suitable if you're used to them on mountain terrain
- Light footwear such as sandals for the evenings
- Lightweight sleeping sheet (silk is perfect); on sale in most CAI rifugi
- Small towel and personal toiletries in small containers
- Mini first aid kit and essential medicines
- Waterproofs – jacket, overtrousers and rucksack cover or a poncho
- Telescopic trekking poles to help wonky knees on steep descents and stream crossings
- Sunglasses, hat, chapstick and high factor sunscreen. For every 1000m you climb the intensity of the sun's UV rays increases

by 10%. Combined with lower levels of humidity and pollution which act as filters elsewhere, and possible snow cover which reflects UV rays, this means you need a higher protection factor sunscreen than at sea level.

- Layers of clothing for conditions from scorching sun to a snow storm: t-shirts and shorts, comfortable long trousers (not jeans), warm fleece, woolly hat and gloves
- High energy snack food such as muesli bars and chocolate
- Maps and guidebook
- Whistle, headlamp or torch (check the batteries!) for emergencies
- Water bottle
- Mobile phone and charger with adaptor
- Supply of euros in cash and a credit/debit card

MAPS

L'Escursionista www.escursionista.it has put together an excellent 1:25,000 scale series of strip maps in a single edition and on waterproof paper: n.8 Alta Via 2 della Valle d'Aosta covers the entire route.

If you prefer larger individual maps, then get hold of their:

- Stage 1: sheet n.11 Valle di Champorcher
- Stages 2–5: sheet n.10 Val di Cogne

- Stages 6–8: sheet n.03 Valgrisenche, Val di Rhemes, Valsavarenche
- Stages 9–10: sheet n.02 La Thuile
- Stages 11–12: sheet n.01 Monte Bianco
- Extension Stages A–D: sheet n.03 Valgrisenche, Val di Rhemes, Valsavarenche

Lastly, Fraternali (www.fraternalieditore.com) does a clear 1:25,000 map, *Parco Nazionale del Gran Paradiso*, handy for Stages 4–6 as well as Stages A–B of the extension.

Maps are usually on sale at bookshops and newspaper kiosks throughout the Gran Paradiso National Park and the Valle d'Aosta, as well as overseas at map outlets and outdoor gear shops.

LANGUAGES AND PLACE NAMES

French was the main language in the valley from the 11th century up until 1861, when Italy was unified. It is still taught and widely spoken, though Italian is prevalent these days. More importantly many inhabitants speak an ancient patois of French-Provençal origin, which includes a wealth of specialised vocabulary for the natural alpine surroundings and pastoral activities.

For these reasons, the spelling of place names on signposts and maps varies considerably and discrepancies are common; a col for instance may be referred to as either *finestra* in the

Italian version or *fenêtre* in French. And the Valle d'Aosta Regional Authority is gradually re-introducing patois toponyms. Be prepared to exercise a little linguistic elasticity!

DOS AND DON'TS

- Find time to get fit before setting out as this will make your trek more enjoyable, not to mention safer.
- Don't overload your rucksack. Apply the golden rule: 10% of your body weight + 2kg. Pop it on the bathroom scales to check. Remember that drinking water and food will add weight; moreover, as the afternoon wears on and that refuge never seems to get any closer, your pack will become inexplicably heavier.
- Familiarise yourself with the stage description and start out as early as possible with extra time up your sleeve to allow for detours due to collapsed bridges, wrong turns and missing signposts. It's not a bad idea to plan for a rest day.
- Check the weather forecast when possible (https://cf.regione.vda.it/) and don't set out in adverse conditions. Rain, wind and snow are tiring and mist can make orientation problematic. During an electrical storm keep away from ridges and metal fixtures and don't shelter under trees or rock overhangs.
- Check out the advice from the CAI experts at https://montagnamicaesicura.it/.
- Tempting though it may be, don't stray from the path, especially not to cut corners. This causes irreparable erosion and damages vegetation. Remember that your

27

The vast valley leading to Col Lauson (Stage 5)

behaviour will encourage others to do the same.

- Carry rubbish away to where it can be disposed of appropriately to save the park and refuge staff time and money. Please don't push it under a rock. Even organic waste (apple cores and orange peel) is best not left lying around as it could upset the diet of animals and birds.

- Be considerate when making a toilet stop. Remember that abandoned huts and rock overhangs could serve as life-saving shelter for someone! If you must use paper or tissues, carry it away; the small bags used by dog owners are handy.

- Under no circumstances are dogs allowed in the park, even on a lead.

- Tempting as it may be to caress a cute baby marmot, wildlife should not be disturbed or handled. Collecting flowers, insects or minerals is strictly forbidden, as are fires and wild camping.

- Always carry extra protective clothing and high energy foods for emergency situations. Remember that the temperature drops an average of 6°C for every 1000 metres you climb.

- Get a handy app like PeakFinder that will help you put names to all those magnificent mountains which will become trail companions.

- Learn the international call for help – see 'Emergencies' below. Don't rely on your mobile phone as there may not be a signal.

- Check the Valle d'Aosta web site for updates regarding the Alta Via 2 as the route may be temporarily diverted in the wake of rockfalls or adverse weather (www.lovevda.it/en/sport/trekking/alte-vie-trails/alta_via_2).

EMERGENCIES

All walkers need health insurance cover. Those from the EU need a European Health Insurance Card (EHIC), while UK residents require a UK Global Insurance Card (GHIC – see www.dh.gov.uk). Holders of both are entitled to free or subsidised emergency treatment in Italy, which has an excellent public health system. Australia has a reciprocal agreement with Italy – see www.medicareaustralia.gov.au. All other nationalities need to take out suitable cover.

In addition, travel insurance to cover an alpine walking holiday is strongly recommended. Membership of alpine clubs includes rescue insurance – see 'Accommodation'.

'Help' is *aiuto* in Italian and 'I need help' is *Ho bisogno di aiuto* (o bee-zon-yoh dee eye-yoo-toh). Experienced refuge staff can always be relied on in emergencies.

Check out the handy GeoResq app (www.cnsas.it/en/georesq/), which can help to determine your geographical location, track your route and send rescue requests.

The international rescue signal may come in handy – the call for help is six signals per minute. These can be visual (such as waving a handkerchief or flashing a torch) or audible (whistling or shouting). They are to be repeated after a one-minute pause. The answer is three visual or audible signals per minute, to be repeated after a one-minute pause. Anyone who sees or hears such a call for help must contact the nearest refuge or police station as quickly as possible.

The general emergency telephone number in Italy is 112, while calls for *soccorso alpino* (mountain rescue) are best made to 118.

USING THIS GUIDE

The AV2 is described here in 12 stages comprising a reasonable day's walking that concludes at accommodation. However, intermediate overnight facilities as well as transport points mean trekkers can customise the route as they wish and plan for longer or shorter days.

The stage headings contain essential information: distance, ascent/descent, grade and time needed.

Distance is given in kilometres – though this is nowhere as important as total ascent/descent (or height gain and loss) given in metres (note: 100m = 328ft).

Grade is an indication of the difficulty of the stage. On the whole, the AV2 rates Grade 2 with a handful of Grade 3 sections – see Stages 5, 7 and 9.

- Grade 1 – a straightforward path with moderate slope
- Grade 2 – a fairly strenuous alpine walk, but not especially difficult
- Grade 3 – experience on alpine terrain is a prerequisite as there may be steep and exposed sections. A head for heights and orientation skills will also come in useful.

Note that adverse weather conditions or snow cover will increase the difficulty of the stage.

Timing is approximate – everyone walks at a different pace. It does not include stops for rests, toilet stops or meals, so always add on a couple of hours to be realistic. Groups should remember that their pace will be dictated by their slowest member.

The sketch maps give an idea of the routes described, together with significant geographical features, but are not intended as substitutes for the commercial maps listed earlier. They are intended to help with pre-trip preparation.

Finally, an Italian-English glossary is provided as an appendix; it contains a wealth of terminology found on maps.

GPX tracks

The GPX tracks for the stages in this guidebook are available to download free at www.cicerone.co.uk/1184/GPX. If you have not bought the book through the Cicerone website, or have bought the book without opening an account, please register your purchase in your Cicerone library to access GPX and update information.

A GPS device is an excellent aid to navigation, but you should also carry a map and compass and know how to use them. GPX files are provided in good faith, but in view of the profusion of formats and devices, neither the author nor the publisher accepts responsibility for their use. We provide files in a single standard GPX format that works on most devices and systems, but you may need to convert files to your preferred format using a GPX converter such as gpsvisualizer.com or one of the many other apps and online converters available.

FURTHER SUGGESTIONS

Walkers concluding the AV2 at Courmayeur will doubtless be extremely fit (if not utterly exhausted) and may like to proceed around the Mont Blanc massif on the popular TMB – see Kev Reynolds, Jonathan Williams and Lesley Williams' *Trekking the Tour du Mont Blanc* (Cicerone, 2024).

Other treks for exploring the Gran Paradiso National Park can be found on the web site www.pngp.it. For shorter day-length walks see the Cicerone guide *Walking in the Gran Paradiso: 30 day walks in the Aosta Valley and Piedmont*.

ALTA VIA 2

The Alta Via 2 begins in the beautiful alpine landscape of Valle di Champorcher. The close-knit local community, with its time-honoured traditions, is descended from herdsmen. Two stories explain its curious name: the first concerns San Porciero, a Roman legionary who took refuge in AD302 near Lago Miserin (Stage 2), where he began to preach. A second attributes the origin to the pigs once bred in the valley and fed on the fruit of oak and beech trees – which all died out after a dramatic temperature drop in the 16th–17th century.

The start point, Chardonney, on the other hand is unrelated to grapes and wine as the name derives from 'agglomeration of thistles'! As well as the bus service from Hône-Bard, Chardonney has grocery shops and accommodation at Hotel Petit Paradis (tel 3440751653, www.petitparadis.it) and Lo Ski Man Gontier (tel 0125 1865237, www.loskiman.it).

Marvellous view to Gran Etret from the path to Gran Collet
(easy alternative, Extension Stage A)

STAGE 1
Chardonney to Rifugio Dondena

Start	Chardonney
Distance	5.8km
Total ascent	750m
Grade	1–2
Time	2hr 30min (opposite direction 2hr)
Note	If Rifugio Péradza in Stage 2 is closed, it's a good idea to extend this stage up to Rifugio Miserin to overnight and thus proceed to Lillaz or Cogne the following day.

Just outside the Gran Paradiso National Park for the moment, this stage entails a straightforward steady climb on good paths, including a lovely stretch of one of the old game tracks. It makes a good introductory stage that is not too strenuous, especially appreciated after the rigours of travelling. That said, it can easily be combined with Stage 2 if desired.

From the bus stop at **Chardonney** (1454m), head up the road to AV2 signposts at a bridge near a car park and Bar del Ponte. Turn L across Torrent Ayasse through scented laburnum trees. Not far up ignore the fork R (the former AV2 route) and keep on the delightful old paved track climbing in wide curves mostly SW and passing under the *telecabina* gondola car cabins. Go up through woodland and pasture clearings dotted with old stone huts. Some 1hr on, you're pointed R for path n.7B and a level stretch. After a ski lift go R to cross two **bridges** (1813m) over Torrent Ayasse then head up to the cluster of farm buildings with a fountain comprising **Alp Créton** (1902m). Now the traverse continues W on a clear path with yellow AV2 arrows, just below a vehicle track. You are rewarded by the lovely sight of Rosa dei Banchi

The old game track leads through pasture

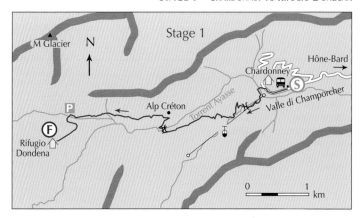

and its snowfield SW. At a **parking area** and cluster of signposts you rejoin the track and recross the stream to climb to the lush flowered pasture basin of Dondena (2097m), well above the tree line. Cut up past old barracks to **Rifugio Dondena** (2192m, **2hr 30min**).

RIFUGIO DONDENA

Although the con-crete building bears no resemblance to the royal hunting lodge it once was, this is amply compensated for by the hospitality and home-style cooking, which, with luck, will include polenta concia corn-meal with melted but-ter and cheese. After-dinner strolls in the

Rifugio Dondena was once a hunting lodge

dark are best confined to the immediate vicinity of the refuge as this used to be a favourite meeting place for witches.

Sleeps 80, accepts credit cards, open late May to mid Sept. Tel 348 6813091, www.miserinespritlibre.it.

STAGE 2
Rifugio Dondena to Rifugio Péradza

Start	Rifugio Dondena
Distance	7.8km
Total ascent	650m
Total descent	300m
Grade	2
Time	3hr (opposite direction 2hr 30min)
Note	Should Rifugio Péradza be closed, count on 3hr more down to Lillaz

Well away from it all now, the AV2 leaves the summer pastures of the Champorcher valley following an age-old route that touches on the sanctuary of Miserin in its lakeside setting. A popular procession is held here every 5 August in honour of Madonna delle Nevi 'Our Lady of the Snows'. The cult originated in the late 4th century after an unseasonal (midsummer!) snowfall in Rome. Participants from the neighbouring valleys of Cogne and Soana throng over the mountains year-in year-out to celebrate their shared history.

Next you face a stiff but unproblematic ascent, possibly across snow, to a broad strategic col, the Finestra di Champorcher, which leads into the Vallon di Cogne on the edge of the national park.

From **Rifugio Dondena** (2192m) follow yellow and black waymarking W along the jeep-width track up the widening valley. Well above the tree line the landscape is brightened by spreads of flowers such as edelweiss, betraying the presence of limestone, and coloured rock such as greenstone. Overhead power lines and pylons are constant companions.

About 1hr on at 2441m, a marginally shorter variant (7B) to Finestra di Champorcher breaks off W, whereas the AV2 keeps L (SW) on a well-used track for Lago Miserin and the refuge. A clear path shortcuts wide curves, leading out onto undulating pastures and a glen housing the lake, sanctuary and **Rifugio Miserin** (2588m, **1hr 30min**) (sleeps 40, accepts credit cards, open mid June to mid Sept, tel 348 6813091, www.miserinespritlibre.it).

A cosy stone building, **Rifugio Miserin** was originally a hospice for travellers such as mine workers crossing to Cogne. Adjacent is the unusually tall and asymmetric church-sanctuary Madonna delle Nevi. Both stand on the shores of lovely Lago Miserin, beneath the gentle contour of 3164m Rosa dei Banchi. The name Rosa derives from 'glacier', whereas Banchi comes from a local word for 'white'.

Cross the front end of the lake by the dam wall and take the clear path across rubble and possible late-lying snow. In gradual ascent W it cuts up the L side of the main valley through masses of bright purple saxifrage to gain **Finestra di Champorcher** (2827m, **1hr**), also referred to as Fenêtre and Colle, opening up between Bec Costazza and Torre Ponton.

Once frequented by witches, medieval travellers, royal hunting parties, miners, soldiers and herders moving their flocks, **Finestra di Champorcher** also hosts power lines though fortunately these do not detract from the enticing views over the vast spread of the snow-capped Gran Paradiso peaks. Drystone walls invite walkers to rest and admire the wide-ranging views, as you'll probably see ibex doing. A stone hut, relic of a former military era, stands to the side of the pass but its precarious state makes it unsuitable for anything

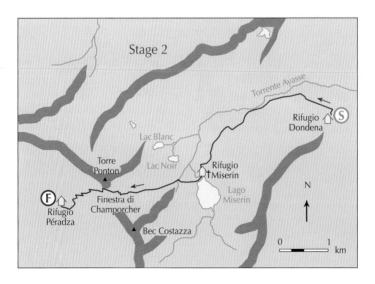

At Finestra di Champorcher

but emergency shelter. Yeld and Coolidge went to the bother of informing their readers that the pass 'was the scene of a skirmish, in September 1799, between the French and Austrian troops', at the time of Napoleon's Second Campaign.

Essentially W the clear path heads down ample Vallon de Urtier in wide curves. The slopes are smothered with oversized violets and yellow creeping avens and pitted with marmot burrows. It is an easy descent past remains of small-scale mining activity to welcoming **Rifugio Péradza** (2526m, **30min**).

RIFUGIO PÉRADZA

Rifugio Péradza is a comfortable establishment

The hut's full name is Sogno di Berdzé al Péradza. Sogno was the name of former owners of this high altitude pasture, Berdzè is local dialect for shepherd or 'berger' in French, while Péradza is a peak due S, its small glacier feeding cascades.

Sleeps 75, accepts credit cards, offers traditional cooking and cosy rooms or a spacious dorm, open mid June to mid Oct. Note that in 2024 the rifugio was closed. Contact Cogne Tourist Office for info (tel 0165 74040).

STAGE 3
Rifugio Péradza to Cogne

Start	Rifugio Péradza
Distance	15km
Total ascent	100m
Total descent	1100m
Grade	2
Time	3hr 40min (opposite direction 4hr 40min)
Note	You can save 40min by taking the Lillaz–Cogne bus

It is a long way down to the valley floor but getting there is enjoyable and the elegant pointed Grivola is visible the whole way. Lacking the crowds of the park's central valleys the Vallon de Urtier has its fair share of chamois, not to mention romping marmots. A further striking feature is the stunning carpet of wildflowers in early summer. (A combination of calcium-rich mica schists produced by the metamorphism of clay sediments alternated with calcareous layers is reputedly responsible for the favourable soil conditions.) Further down are light conifer woods. At the day's end are the friendly settlements of Lillaz and Cogne where a good range of creature comforts – and transport if needed – are on offer.

From **Rifugio Péradza** (2526m) a brief stretch of jeep track leads downhill to where the AV2 path resumes L (W). Marshy terrain means summertime concentrations of white ranunculus and pasque flowers, and several streams to be crossed by bridges.

A brief climb is followed by a long, fairly level and especially scenic stretch high above a farm road. The steep mountainsides opposite below Mont Creyaz were the site of intensive mining until the 1970s. Alpenrose and juniper shrubs, not to mention black vanilla orchids, precede a light wood of Arolla pine and larch – shade at last! The path eventually bears L (S) and yellow arrows point the winding way down past a park ranger's hut. Shortly you cross a bridge in **Vallon de Bardoney** (2140m, **1hr 30min**) where the stream descends in a dramatic series of cascades. Here you turn R, joined by the path from Alpe Bardoney. Zigzags through conifer woods lead to a clearing and intersection with a farm track. Close

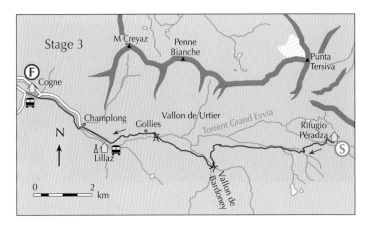

to Torrent Grand Eyvia now, you quickly cross a wooden bridge R then keep L below the tiny hamlet of **Gollies** (1830m). The valley narrows and immense slabs of glacially smoothed rock are passed above the Lillaz waterfalls. Follow AV2 way-marks carefully on this stretch. Water pipes accompany the path through pretty woodland, down to a small power plant and the road at the lovely village of **Lillaz** (1617m, **1hr 30min**) with splendid views to Mont Blanc.

The leisurely path continues down the flowered flanks of Vallon de Urtier

Mont Blanc itself can be glimpsed from Lillaz

Lillaz offers a free summer bus to Cogne, groceries, cafés, accommodation at B&B Jeantet Abele (tel 0165 749129), Hotel Ondezana (tel 0165 74248, www.hotelondezana.it), Hotel L'Arolla (tel 0165 74052, https://hotelarolla.it/) and Camping Les Salasses (tel 347 1248766, www.campingcogne.it).

If you're not taking the bus, from the car park head down the cycle track parallel to the road. At **Champlong** the AV2 turns L over a bridge then down through pleasant woods flanking the torrent. The banal-looking shrine passed shortly is dated 1842 and bears the surprising announcement that the Bishop of Aosta conceded sinners a number of days' indulgence for every Ave Maria recited there. As the track finally joins the road, detour briefly to the adjacent footbridge to look down on the amazing striated smoothed rock and the powerful, whirling river at your feet.

You walk into the nearby centre of **Cogne** (1540m, **40min**).

COGNE

This erstwhile mining and lace-making village has plenty of grocery shops, excellent bakeries, an ATM, daily buses to Aosta as well as a helpful tourist office (tel 0165 74040) in the main square and beautifully kept old timber and stone buildings.

The vast range of accommodation includes budget Ostello La Mine (a 10min walk uphill from the bridge, rooms and dorm, accepts credit cards) (tel 0165 74445, www.ostellocogne.it) and Residence Chateau Royal (tel 0165 751912, www.residencechateauroyal.com). For a camping ground press on to Valnontey by bus or on foot – see Stage 4.

STAGE 4

Cogne to Rifugio Vittorio Sella

Start	Cogne
Distance	8.5km
Total ascent	1050m
Grade	1–2
Time	3hr 20min (opposite direction 2hr 30min)
Note	You can save 50min by taking the Cogne–Valnontey bus

Beginning with a pleasant stroll past flowered meadows and through woodland, the AV2 then reaches the tiny settlement of Valnontey, where a handful of hotels offer accommodation. (This opening section can be covered by free summer bus.) Flower enthusiasts will enjoy a break at Valnontey to stroll around the 10,000m² Giardino Botanico Alpino 'Paradisia' which boasts thousands of labelled species. Afterwards the trail climbs steadily on a former game track to one of the park's most popular refuges, in a vast valley above the tree line where wildlife can be observed all year round.

From the centre of **Cogne** (1540m) the AV2 follows the road Rue Grand Paradis (signposted for Valnontey) SSW. It's a pleasant stroll along the pavement flanking the Prati di Sant'Orso. These manicured meadows were named after Saint Ursus, an Irish monk believed to have banished snakes from the valley so the land could be cultivated in safety.

After the last hotel and a bridge, the AV2 forks L to follow a path through conifer wood above the road. Further along, ignore two consecutive underpasses R (for winter cross-country skiers), and keep to the L of the tarmac, over old rockfalls. You finally cross the road R near a camping ground and take a lane along the river. You soon pass a car park, bus stop and café to reach **Valnontey** (1666m, **50min**).

Accommodation at Valnontey includes Affittacamere La Clicca (tel 349 1568661 or 0165 74157, https://affittacamerelacli.wixsite.com), Meublè Lou Tsantelet (tel 0165 74635, www.loutsantelet.it) and campsites such as Lo Stambecco (tel 0165 74152, www.campeggiolostambecco.it).

The old game track leading to Rifugio Vittorio Sella

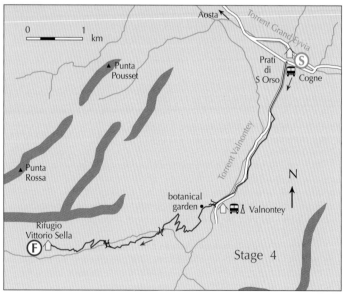

Aosta

Torrent Grand Eyvia

Punta Pousset

Prati di S Orso

Cogne

Punta Rossa

Torrent Valnontey

botanical garden

Valnontey

Rifugio Vittorio Sella

N

Stage 4

0   1
km

Cross to the W side of Torrent Valnontey, where path n.18 climbs past the **botanical garden**. You head towards a waterfall and up the mountainside on the wide easy curves of an old mule track. After a larch wood, the last shade you'll enjoy today, the path crosses a timber **bridge** onto open terrain inhabited by marmots amidst a series of summer farms. Views improve considerably towards the glaciers S. After a third **bridge** that sees you switch back to the R side of the river, the AV2 climbs in wide zigzags and finally enters a vast basin. Here stands an old photogenic hunting lodge, now home to the park rangers, and not far on you come to the former stables which have been transformed into hospitable **Rifugio Vittorio Sella** (2588m, **2hr 30min**).

RIFUGIO VITTORIO SELLA

Lovely Lago Lauson is a short stroll from Rifugio Vittorio Sella

The hut was named after a highly acclaimed pioneer alpine photographer from the 1800s whose black and white masterpieces are unparalleled. Due W, tomorrow's goal, the notch of Col Lauson, is clearly visible. Make the effort to take an evening stroll S to nearby Lago Lauson to watch the ibex and chamois.

Sleeps 150, CAI, open June to end Sept, accepts credit cards. Tel 0165 74310, www.rifugiosella.com.

STAGE 5

Rifugio Vittorio Sella to Eaux Rousses

Start	Rifugio Vittorio Sella
Distance	16.5km
Total ascent	750m
Total descent	1650m
Grade	2–3
Time	5hr 45min (opposite direction 6hr 30min)

A magnificent, rewarding traverse and important segment of the AV2, this leads to the highest point on the whole of the trek, Col Lauson, which also happens to be the highest non-glaciated pass accessible to walkers in the Gran Paradiso National Park. Needless to say, a monumental knee-destroying descent follows! The landscape is surprisingly varied with both woods and vast grassed and debris-strewn mountainsides, accompanied by breathtaking, sweeping panoramas. Wildlife in all shapes and sizes is equally numerous on both sides of the pass while on the desolate eastern flanks human beings are few and far between.

The sole difficulty concerns the approach to Col Lauson: the terrain in its immediate vicinity is unstable and steep and inadvisable for inexperienced walkers. In early summer this sheltered western side tends to be snow-bound and may be icy, while by mid to late summer it is generally clear. Check at the refuge if in doubt. In any case, carry plenty of drinking water today.

Leave **Rifugio Vittorio Sella** (2588m) on path n.18 and head W up the grassed slopes. The gentle gradient and ample width tell you it was another of the king's mid-19th century tracks. After a stretch alongside the stream, ignore the turn-off R for Punta Rossa and continue into a final flat upper valley. The slopes are covered by shattered rock debris, scattered with saxifrage and clumps of alpine buttercups.

In this lunar landscape the climb becomes decidedly stiffer and numerous zigzags cut up to a brief gully and a 'false' col (not the actual pass yet!). This precedes a short exposed passage with reassuring cable where a sure foot is essential on the crumbly terrain. It is then only a short diagonal climb to **Col Lauson**

The highest pass on the AV2

(3299m, **2hr 15min**), otherwise known as Col du Loson (from 'lose', the slippery black shale used locally for roofing slabs). For Yeld and Coolidge last century it was 'probably the highest path traversed by horses and not leading over a glacier in the Alps'. Views are partially limited here, although you can see the impressive Torre del Grande San Pietro SE back over Valnontey.

Side trip to Punta del Tuf (30min return)

For walkers with climbing experience, the ascent of adjoining 3393m Punta del Tuf is suggested for a vaster panorama. In the absence of snow or ice, the peak can be reached via the easy crest S. The view even takes in the distant Matterhorn and Monte Rosa NE. The crest running SW from here to Gran Serra features unusual bright to pale yellows, because of outcrops of gypsum-bearing limestones which gave rise to the name Tuf.

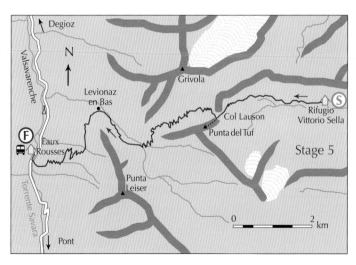

The final approach to Col Lauson

Main route continued

The initial part of the descent, NNW at first, may be icy but by midsummer is usually clear and straightforward. This vast desolate valley has debris-strewn slopes which give way to meagre grass populated by chamois, ibex and marmots further down. A huge knoll (at approximately 3000m) affords a glimpse S of the Gran Paradiso peak, not to mention massive Mont Taou Blanc SW on the opposite side of Valsavarenche.

The path winds its way almost lazily downhill, in the wide curves suitable for the horseborne hunting parties. Soon after a second prominent knoll (2700m) carpeted with tiny bright gentians, the path heads decisively but briefly S, and the craggy snowbound pyramid of the Herbetet comes into sight SSE. After a bridge the path contours high above grazing flats with the ubiquitous marmots. Shrub vegetation including alpenrose has colonised the valley here. It is not far to **Levionaz en Bas** (2303m, **2hr 15min**) or Livionaz-Desot, old farm buildings converted to park rangers' premises. Drinking water available. It stands on the very edge of a glacially formed platform, with a dramatic plunge into Valsavarenche.

Heading SW the AV2 moves into the shade of a beautiful larch and Arolla pine wood. It is alive with squirrels and nutcrackers while the undergrowth is thick with cowberry and bearberry shrubs. On a long level section the path seems to be unsure whether or not to descend until it crosses a stream. The final stretch is swept by avalanches in winter, as demonstrated by a debris fan scattered with broken trees. At last a walled-in path through fields takes you over the bridge spanning the Torrente Savara to **Eaux Rousses** (1666m, **1hr 15min**).

EAUX ROUSSES

The name Eaux Rousses refers to the red rock at the rear of the hamlet, stained by the water that trickles down from a spring containing iron ore.

This is a cluster of old stone buildings including the cosy guesthouse Hostellerie du Paradis with rooms and an excellent restaurant (accepts credit cards, tel 0165 905972, www.hostellerieduparadis.it). A similarly priced alternative 1.2km down the road is Camping Grivola with simple rooms, meals and groceries (accepts credit cards, open Apr to Sept, tel 0165 905743, www.campinghotelgrivola.com). Buses run year-round to Aosta.

Note: to vary the AV2 using the extension, leave the main route here and take the summer bus 5km upvalley to Pont.

EXTENSION ROUTE

Four days are spent on this suggested extension which skips Stages 6 and 7. Leave the official AV2 route at Eaux Rousses and head up the road to Pont (5km by summer bus). Then it's uphill via Pian del Nivolet, up to Col Rosset then Rifugio Benevolo, before traversing via Col Bassac Déré then Rifugio Bezzi and down to Valgrisenche, to resume the AV2 during Stage 8. Difficulty varies between Grades 2 and 3 as there are several narrow tricky stretches, though all effort is amply compensated with superb views.

The Gran Paradiso can be admired near Gran Collet (Stage A)

EXTENSION STAGE A
Pont to Col del Nivolet

Start	Valsavarenche
Distance	10.5km
Total ascent	1010m
Total descent	450m
Grade	2
Time	4hr 40min

A hefty relentless ascent worth every puff and metre concludes at the 2832m Gran Collet and walkers are rewarded with a superb uninterrupted view over the Gran Paradiso peak with its snowfield and neighbours. Be aware that the top section could be obstructed by snow drifts in early summer – ask at Pont. This is followed by a stroll over the marvellous Pian del Nivolet (from 'snow'), a vast altopiano alias ancient glacial trough lying 2300–2500m above sea level. It is renowned for the unrivalled spectacle in early summer when it is transformed into a sea of white and yellow by the buttercup *ranunculus pyrenaeus* and pasque flowers.

Thankfully a link road to Pont proposed in the 1960s related to a hydroelectric project never materialised, leaving the peaceful plateau for the enjoyment of livestock, marmots, walkers and other wildlife.

An easier, shorter route (3hr) excluding the Gran Collet takes the path via Croix de l'Arolley – see below.

Pont accommodation includes Hotel Gran Paradiso (tel 0165 95454, www.hotelgparadiso.com), Rifugio Tetras Lyre (see below) and Camping Pont Breuil (tel 351 7128603, www.campingpontbreuil.com).

From the car park at **Pont** (1960m) walk through to the river but don't cross the bridge. Go R (S) on the parallel lane up Vallone de la Seyvaz for 15min to the next bridge (link L to Rifugio Tetras Lyre (accepts credit cards, open mid June to mid Sept, tel 335 6001921 or 348 6723645, www.rifugiotetraslyre.it).

Here a narrow signposted path (2A) breaks off R. The climb is immediately stiff and the path narrow but good. Bearing almost imperceptibly SSW it heads for abandoned Alpe de Seyvaz (2358m), home to marmots and a park ranger hut.

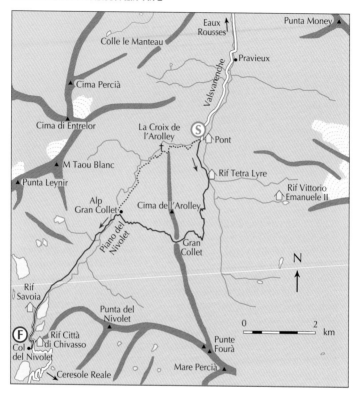

At the head of the valley the Grand Etret glacier is visible, overshadowed by the Denti del Broglio.

Turning W further on, you climb through a series of grassy basins, many of which will be occupied by ibex females and their inquisitive young who spy on visitors from giddy outcrops. Iron steps and rods help you up steep rocks. At the last ample terrace preceding the pass, visible now, a photographic stop is called for as the view is partially obscured from the pass itself. From ESE to NE is a stunning sweep taking in Ciarforon, Tresenta, Rifugio Vittorio Emanuele II beneath Gran Paradiso itself, then Piccolo Paradiso and Becca di Montandayne.

The final stretch cuts up the right flank of a snow-specked slope to the ample saddle of **Gran Collet** (2832m, **2hr 30min**), where a squawking flock of alpine choughs awaits your crumbs. While not on a par with the preceding valley, intriguing new views open up W-S dominated by Mont Taou Blanc WNW, and Punta Basei WSW, interspersed with small glacier and snow pockets.

The path heads WNW down a dirt slope and back onto grassy terrain bejewelled with piercing blue gentians and riddled with marmot burrows as well as tarns. Where the path as such disappears, cairns point the way across the grassy slopes easily down to the ruined huts of **Alpe Gran Collet** (2403m, **40min**) where you turn L joined by the direct path from Pont.

A short distance along SW, the broad path climbs briefly and bridges cross the meanders of the stream among densely flowered high-altitude meadows. Further up you join the surfaced road. Close by are two sizeable lakes, then **Rifugio Savoia** (2532m) (Sleeps 38, credit cards accepted, open mid June to late Sept, tel 0165 94141, www.rifugiosavoia.com). Originally one of the king's hunting lodges, it is now a welcoming refuge with a traditional restaurant.

The rewarding views on the climb to Gran Collet

The lakes at Col del Nivolet

Not far up the road and off to the L stands quieter solar-powered **Rifugio Città di Chivasso** (2604m) (closed at the time of writing, tel 0165 905703 for info).

The actual pass, **Col del Nivolet** (2612m, **1hr 20min**) is only a matter of minutes up the road, and, together with the marvellous angle onto Punta Basei W from here, a whole new world of stunning mountain ranges – most notably the three Levanne peaks SSE bordering France and its Vanoise National Park and lakes – opens up at your feet.

Easy alternative via La Croix de l'Arolley (3hr to Col del Nivolet)

At **Pont** (1960m) take the signposted path (n.3) from the rear of Hotel Gran Paradiso. It climbs easily W through larch wood and alpenrose close to a waterfall before the gradient increases dramatically as you zigzag up the steep escarpment on a reinforced path to the prominent old wooden cross, **La Croix de l'Arolley** (2310m).

Brief ups and downs lead across expanses of rock polished by the slow passage of an ancient glacier and lovely picnic spots present themselves by a gushing torrent as you head SW. Keeping to the L side of the open valley, Piano del Nivolet, the next landmark is the stone skeleton of the buildings of **Alpe Gran Collet** (2403m) just off the path, and here you join up with the main itinerary.

EXTENSION STAGE B

Col del Nivolet to Rifugio Benevolo

Start	Col del Nivolet
Distance	10km
Total ascent	650m
Total descent	900m
Grade	2–3
Time	4hr

A short stroll above Col del Nivolet is the Piani di Rosset plateau – a stunning expanse of lakes and pasture amidst breathtaking scenery from the Tre Levanne to the Ciarforon to Gran Paradiso line-up, with Mont Taou Blanc and massive Punta Basei close by. The climb continues to Col Rosset, an ice-free age-old passage to neighbouring Val di Rhêmes. The ensuing descent is the sole section likely to involve any difficulty – a steep detritus-covered flank, a little unstable especially with late-lying snow. The walk concludes at well-run Rifugio Benevolo, always a pleasant experience. An added attraction of upper Val di Rhêmes is the spectacular Granta Parei peak.

On the roadside a tad below the southern side of the **Col del Nivolet** pass (2612m), path n.3C turns up NNW over a rise. (If you start out from **Rifugio Savoia** head uphill on popular Col Leynir path n.3B but only as far as **Alpage Riva** (2590m) with its flowing drinking fountains, then branch L to quickly slot into the main route.) Yellow arrows lead over grassy terrain up onto the **Piani di Rosset**, where a short veer E–N proceeds between the two major lakes, **Lago Rosset** and **Lago Leytaz**, the outlook inspiring to say the least.

A steady but short-lived ascent N begins among thick clumps of edelweiss, proceeding along a wide, shiny corridor of mica schists. Snow lies in depressions around the path and chamois seem to enjoy lazing in it. More tarns (Laghi di Chanavey) lie along the way to the base of an escarpment. The final 150m uphill is a series of tight and exacting zigzags crossing multicoloured bands of dark grey-brown, greenstone and pink-tinged limestone.

Col Rosset (3023m, **2hr**) is quite something, with generous views in all directions.

For the descent NW, path n.13A disappears beneath your boots down the initially steep scree-earth slope. Tricky and a little exposed and guided by occasional yellow markings, it embarks on a wide curve L, then zigzags. The going soon becomes a little easier on the knees as you return to stable grassed terrain. Amidst flowers and marmots the path veers N, keeping to the R side of Vallon de Grand Vaudalaz and its gushing stream, and heads for the old farm buildings of **Grand Vaudalaz** (2338m, **1hr 10min**). But just before reaching them, your narrow path (n.13A) branches L to cross the main stream.

You now climb diagonally W across mixed rock flows. The dry hillside is alive with grasshoppers and the scree is thick with pink-violet felted adenostyle flowers.

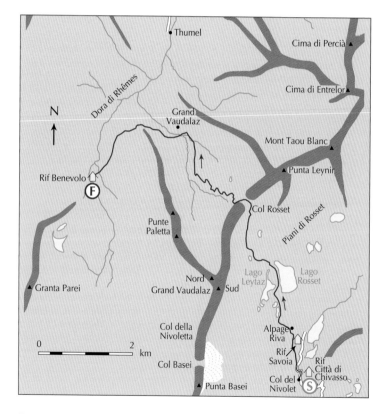

A shoulder at 2417m comes with the reward of the wonderful spectacle of light-coloured peaks and ice that crown the head of the Val di Rhêmes, in addition to an aerial view of the valley floor.

Over rolling pasture and hillocks now, guided by cairns, you proceed SW to the refuge, visible ahead on an outcrop. You'll probably lose sight of the path as the cattle, which belong to nearby Alpe Lavassey, usually manage to obliterate it, but waymarking is frequently renewed. If you don't manage to come out on the 4WD track just below the refuge, wander over the hillside until you spot a convenient stock descent route to **Rifugio Benevolo** (2285m, **50min**).

RIFUGIO BENEVOLO

Welcoming Rifugio Benevolo

Named after an entomologist from Turin, this hospitable old-style refuge is run by staff who know the area like the back of their hand and score high on catering. A regular diner is the sleek fox who drops in after dark for scraps. If you have time to spare, take the easy path leading to the beautiful upper valley to the source of the Dora di Rhêmes torrent beneath glaciers. In the early morning the Granta Parei, whose name comes from 'great wall', is at its best, illuminated to perfection.

Sleeps 48, open mid June to mid Sept, accepts credit cards. Tel 0165 936143 or 345 4238692, https://rifugiobenevolo.com.

EXTENSION STAGE C
Rifugio Benevolo to Rifugio Bezzi

Start	Rifugio Benevolo
Distance	10km
Total ascent	850m
Total descent	860m
Grade	2–3
Time	5hr + 1hr optional summit

This is a hard stage to beat. Once away from the huts, there are few other walkers and you find yourself in wild desolate valleys edged with inspiring and sobering seas of ice.

An optional exceptional summit with 360° views is described. The dizzy perch of Becca della Traversière became accessible for walkers due to the ongoing retreat of ice on both sides of the Col Bassac Déré pass. Mid to late summer is the best time when snow cover should be at a manageable minimum.

From **Rifugio Benevolo** (2285m) follow wàymarking (n.13D) down to the stone bridge across the river. The clear path climbs diagonally NNW to the old farm buildings of Sotses or Sauches (2313m), then sharp L (S). You pass a turn-off for the Granta Parei lake and keep R up the steep zigzags to the crest where there are magnificent views E to the Gran Paradiso. This leads SW into the stone desert plateau, Comba di Golettaz, following cairns along the L bank of the stream. Below the triangular point of the Granta Parei, the wrinkled surface of the Ghiacciaio di Golettaz forms the uppermost banks of grey **Lago Goletta** (2699m). This is an unworldly spot where huge grey ravens hang out.

Stepping stones cross the lake outlet and the yellow-marked path continues up the R side of the valley. You climb steadily, alternating between debris and snow. The flowers are surprisingly abundant in midsummer, and the varied colourful rocks, including limestone, host blue Mount Cenis bellflowers, white alpine mouse-ear and yellow daisies – an irresistible attraction for butterflies. The final stretch to the pass crosses a steep snow field, where you need to watch your step. You eventually step out at the narrow saddle of **Col Bassac Déré** (3082m, **3hr**), a breathtaking

Lago Goletta is a superb spot

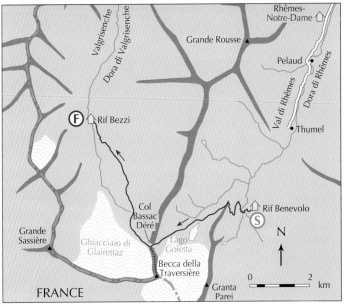

spot. A massive expanse of ice, Ghiacciaio di Glairettaz, completely fills the next valley and above it is immense dark Grande Sassière W. Back E the line-up extends from the Gran Paradiso to the Grivola NE.

Optional ascent to Becca della Traversière (1hr return)

This ascent is straightforward in good conditions but on the way back down the path will feel more exposed. It is recommended for experienced walkers with a good head for heights.

From **Col Bassac Déré** take the unnumbered path L (due S) and around to a saddle. A clear path winds up the crest to the top of **Becca della Traversière** (3337m) on the Italian-French border. The view from here is simply stunning. Seas of white

The path to Becca della Traversière is breathtaking

extend in all directions, and over them, with any luck, you will be rewarded by the sight of Mont Blanc NNW and the Matterhorn NW. Take the descent slowly the same way back to **Col Bassac Déré**.

Main route continued
The narrow dirt path (n.12C) drops R (NW) on loose terrain and makes its way towards the edge of the glacier, then skirts above it to head N. The descent is gradual and problem free. Endless tongues of snow are crossed below Punta Bassac Déré then Punta Bassac Sud in a desolate, silent, high-altitude landscape, morainic for the most part. A rainbow of rocks is underfoot – greens, purples and greys – supporting myriad flowers.

After a good hour the valley narrows and concertina crevasses on the vast body of ice announce a change of gradient. The path reaches the edge of an escarpment, still at around 2850m, and grassy terrain at last. The refuge is visible below now, while N is the Testa del Ruitor with Mont Chateau Blanc to its R. The way drops quickly NNW, sometimes on loose scree. The terrain is thickly flowered and a couple of side torrents are crossed or forded. Powerful crashing waterfalls are at hand.

Set among emerald pastures is welcoming **Rifugio Bezzi** (2284m, **2hr**).

RIFUGIO BEZZI

The smaller wing of the hut dates back to the 1925 but the refuge boasts a spacious modern wing with all mod cons. Solar-heated showers come free of charge. You are well fed here and can enjoy polenta con spezzatino (stewed meat).

Sleeps 80, accepts credit cards, open mid June to mid Sept. Tel 0165 97129 or 340 8123364, www.rifugiobezzi.com.

EXTENSION STAGE D
Rifugio Bezzi to Planaval

Start	Rifugio Bezzi
Distance	17km (less by bus)
Total ascent	310m
Total descent	1035m
Grade	1–2
Time	4hr 15min

After a straightforward enjoyable ramble down a valley important for sheep and woodland, you follow the edge of the dammed lake, Lago Beauregard, in Valgrisenche. This concludes at the principal village (also known as Valgrisenche) where you pick up the main AV2 route. En route is a string of inviting places to stay overnight and dine, should you opt for shorter days.

Rifugio Bezzi

Leave **Rifugio Bezzi** (2284m) past the hut's cableway on path n.12 downhill due N on the R side of the Dora di Valgrisenche stream. The valley opens up gradually with new mountains coming into view. In the vicinity of ruined huts (Alpage Saxe Savoie, 2030m) overgrown by masses of rosebay willowherb, a vehicle track is joined.

Further down as the wood starts, ignore the **1848m turnoff** R for n.9A to Rifugio Chalet de l'Epée (unless you opt for the 500m/1hr 30min ascent to the lovely family-run hut and conclusion of Stage 7). At a **1784m junction** near a summer eatery, keep R to the abandoned church and hamlet of **Uselères** (1785m, **1hr 15min**) and cosy B&B and restaurant Giason (tel 334 7115984, www.giasson.it).

The remaining 6.5km to Valgrisenche are along a quiet narrow road above the eastern edge of **Lago Beauregard**. The lake was created in the 1950s for

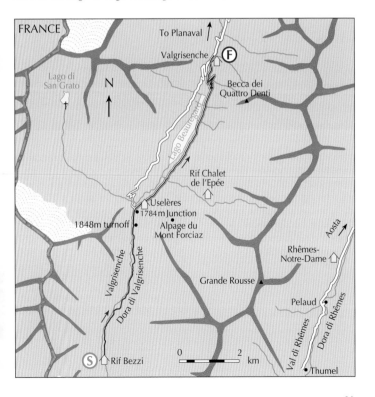

61

Valgrisenche

hydroelectricity by damming the valley and flooding six villages; buildings can be glimpsed when the water level is low. The road is partially surfaced but it is closed to motorised traffic which uses the opposite bank. At the far end of the dam wall, the road zigzags valleywards and you can pick up the AV2 shortcuts. Down at the sports ground, tarmac leads over a bridge to the main road where you go R to the village of **Valgrisenche** (1664m, **1hr 30min**) (tourist info, bus, ATM, groceries, cafès and restaurants. Accommodation at B&B Lo Souvenir (tel 345 9155087, www.bblosouvenir.it)).

See Stage 8 for the remaining 1hr 30min to Planaval on the main AV2 route.

STAGE 6

Eaux Rousses to Rhêmes-Notre-Dame

Start	Eaux Rousses
Distance	16km
Total ascent	1350m
Total descent	1300m
Grade	2
Time	6hr 40min (opposite direction 6hr 30min)
Note	The day's load can be shortened marginally – by 30min – if you opt for an overnight stay at Rifugio delle Marmotte.

Another lengthy traverse with stunning views and hefty ups and downs, this stage leads through fascinating landscapes dotted with an old hunting lodge, alpages and lakes. The wild, broad valleys on both sides of lofty Col di Entrelor are the playground of chamois and ibex, as well as marmots and foxes. Extra care is needed on the steep north-facing descent where snow cover is feasible in early summer. Apart from welcoming Rifugio delle Marmotte, half an hour from the stage end, there are no intermediate stopovers so you drop to a valley for the night's stay at Bruil, Rhêmes-Notre-Dame.

From the main road at **Eaux Rousses** (1666m), the AV2 turns off the asphalt up through the cluster of houses, and to the rear of the Hostellerie du Paradis. Close at hand is the trickling waterfall over the rust-coloured rock that gave the hamlet its name. A stiff climb N for the most part leads through abandoned terraces and into dense conifer wood, mostly spruce and larch and home to industrious squirrels and even lone chamois. As well as bilberries, the undergrowth includes the rare twinflower. The wood finally gives way to pasture and wide curves take you to the grassy flat of **Orvieille** (2164m, **1hr 30min**), literally 'Old Alp'.

> The **long building** belongs to the park nowadays, but it once hosted royal hunting parties and was a regular site for encampments, even boasting a telegraph line. Views here offer a good range of Valsavarenche peaks, as well as a glimpse of the imposing Gran Combin far away N.

Heading S now you follow the fence alongside the buildings where there is drinking water, then climb to a summer farm, where you'll probably have to pick your way through mud. Several more typical stone-roofed huts and wooden crosses are passed on dry grassy hillsides 'infested' by carline thistles and crickets, with acrobatic swallows overhead. As the trees are left behind, the outlook opens up onto the Gran Paradiso SE, not to mention the elegant point of the Grivola NE. Moving SW you gradually enter Vallone dei Laghi, its flanks bright red with bilberry shrubs above golden larches in late summer. The path continues effortlessly to **Lac Djouan** (2515m, **1hr 10min**), a

Lac Djouan with Col de Entrelor

peaceful shallow tarn, a perfect picnic spot and worthwhile destination in itself. In addition to alpine charr, a type of salmon, and wild ducks, this area is also home to herds of both chamois and ibex – scan the nearby crests with your binoculars.

Skirt the N bank of the lake and ignore a fork L for Valle delle Meyes. The AV2 keeps R (SW) to **Lac Noir** (2650m). Despite its name it is deep green and occupies a steep-sided basin where the silence is broken only by tiny, twittering ground-nesting birds. The path takes wide curves beneath Cime di Gollien (local dialect for 'small body of water', a reference to the underlying lakes). Amidst hardy alpine cushion flowers, it then narrows as the old game track peters out and a final stretch over rubble leads to the airy pass **Col di Entrelor** (3007m, **1hr 30min**), 'between two alps'. It offers a glimpse of Mont Blanc (distant NW), while nearby S is Cima Percià (pierced), then SW dark grey Becca Tsambellinaz.

Accompanied by masses of white alpine mouse-ear, the path drops steeply W down rough terrain, exposed and possibly snow-covered or muddy. But you are soon back on a decent if narrow path with a more reasonable gradient and enter the immense and desolate Vallone di Entrelor. The small glacier beneath Cima di Entrelor S is responsible for the moraine which spills downwards forming long barriers. Ample grassy flats are soon reached with the promise of grazing chamois and romping marmots.

Stick to the R side of the valley all the way to the curious vaulted huts of **Plan de la Feya** (2403m), 'plain of the sheep'. The immense, pointed Grande Rousse is straight ahead WNW. Here the AV2 turns decisively L (W) down a wider path towards the stream. The first larch trees appear as the path follows the R bank of the stream to another flowered pasture flat and a knoll (Entrelor, 2143m, **2hr**) with **Rifugio delle Marmotte** (sleeps 12, open mid June to mid Sept, tel 389 3488785, www.rifugiodellemarmotte.it). The beautifully renovated buildings are set on the lip of Val di Rhêmes.

The path wanders delightfully, heading NW through larch woods, golden in late summer with brilliant russet undergrowth, and with bilberries for early walkers. You descend in easy zigzags, past an excellent lookout to the majestic

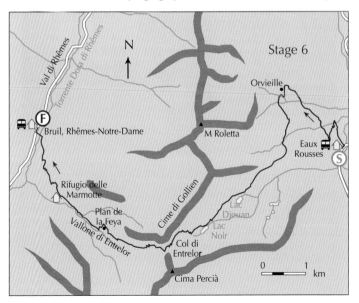

limestone Granta Parei SSW at the head of the valley. Diagonally beneath the prominent rock dubbed Castel di Cucco, the path eventually exits on the valley floor, where only a bridge separates you from the peaceful village of **Bruil, Rhêmes-Notre-Dame** (1723m, **30min**).

BRUIL, RHÊMES-NOTRE-DAME

Bruil, Rhêmes-Notre-Dame

The village boasts shops and a year-round bus service to Aosta, not to mention a delightful 18th-century church where a sundial reminds passers-by that 'Nos jours passent comme l'ombre' ('Our days pass by like the shade').

Sleep and eat at Chez Lydia (tel 0165 936103, www.hotelchezlidia.it) or B&B at Agriturismo Lo Sabot (tel 0165 936150, https://agriturismolosabot.wordpress.com). At nearby Chavaney (1.5km) is a National Park Visitor Centre with a stuffed lammergeier, one of the valley's last specimens from the times when the locals were paid to shoot them. (Note: Rhêmes-Notre-Dame is used to refer to the grouping of villages in upper Val di Rhêmes. Bruil is the principal settlement.)

STAGE 7

Rhêmes-Notre-Dame to Rifugio Chalet de l'Epée

Start	Rhêmes-Notre-Dame
Distance	7.4km
Total ascent	1150m
Total descent	500m
Grade	2–3
Time	4hr (opposite direction 3hr 15min)

This rewarding traverse links lovely Val di Rhêmes with quiet, rural Valgrisenche. Even though the AV2 leaves the national park today, wildlife is still plentiful. (They can't read the signs.) A good path sets out uphill, becoming a little tricky in the higher reaches due to unstable terrain where fixed ropes help walkers. Late-lying snow could make this more difficult. On one hand it is a rather long and occasionally monotonous 1150m ascent to cross Col Fenêtre; but on the other, this is a relatively short day and the stage concludes at a homely rifugio run by a hospitable local family.

From the centre of **Bruil, Rhêmes-Notre-Dame** (1723m) the AV2 follows the road for a short way N, branching off L at a car park and across meadows. Needless to say it is not long before the climb begins in earnest. Heading W, it goes through larch then past a prominent outcrop. The clear path traverses steep dry hillsides enlivened by hosts of butterflies. Unusual stone huts with broad roofing slabs are encountered at **Alpage Torrent** (2179m, **1hr 10min**), all but blending into the boulders that serve as walls.

Tight zigzags climb through densely flowered marmot territory on the way towards rubble-strewn slopes. The gradient becomes steeper and steeper and the terrain more challenging as grass is left behind. Several sections of rope help you clamber up the final tiring metres to **Col Fenêtre** (2840m, **2hr**).

A scenic spot, **Col Fenêtre** includes views to Testa del Ruitor (NW) with the Mont Blanc massif beyond and, looking E, Gran Paradiso and the village of Bruil some giddy 1100m below on the valley floor. More often than not the pass is occupied by ibex, so approach with care as they unfailingly dislodge loose stones if spurred to sudden flight.

Splendid Grande Rousse dominates the valley

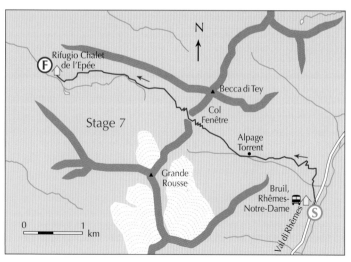

In descent, the gradient is gentler and the path bears R at first across a rock and earth mix, bearing generally W in the shade of a vast brown ridge culminating in Becca di Tey. The opposite flanks consist of light grey scree spills from elegant outrunners of Grande Rousse. This area is home to eagles. Following a stream, you drop into an idyllic emerald green pasture basin inhabited by noisy flocks of yellow-beaked alpine choughs. Further down a livestock track is joined to reach **Rifugio Chalet de l'Epée** (2370m, **50min**).

RIFUGIO CHALET DE L'EPÉE

The original building, a shepherd's hut called Chalet l'Epère, took its name from *pierres* or stones, abundant here. A comfortable stay is guaranteed in this family-run hut. You'll dine on polenta with fontina cheese and butter from the nearby farm, if not home-made sausages and *tartiflette* potato and cheese fry-up. A fitting conclusion is a miniature glass of grappa from the custodian's collection. The outlook ranges over the western flanks of Valgrisenche, where the prominent Ruitor peak stands out and its glacier glimpsed.

Sleeps 80, accepts credit cards, open mid June to late Sept. Tel 0165 97215, www.rifugioepee.com.

Rifugio Chalet de l'Epée

STAGE 8
Rifugio Chalet de l'Epée to Planaval

Start	Rifugio Chalet de l'Epée
Distance	13.5km
Total ascent	50m
Total descent	900m
Grade	1–2
Time	3hr 20min (opposite direction 4hr 30min)

This easy stage drops across medium altitude pasture with masses of wildflowers along with views towards the Testa del Ruitor and its glacier entourage. Down on the floor of rural Valgrisenche, the AV2 alternates farm tracks with short stretches of tarmac. The main village of Valgrisenche has good facilities including groceries and a year-round bus to Aosta, and there are several accommodation options during the stage. The day's final destination is a tiny hamlet with a comfortable hotel geared to walkers' needs.

Valgrisenche has an age-old tradition of hand weaving local Rosset sheep's wool into a fabric known as *drap*, which is crafted into scarves, garments and shawls. Products and looms can be admired in the village.

Note: This stage is a good chance to rest ahead of the demanding stage tomorrow, and stock up on groceries as you'll be self-catering tomorrow night at the unmanned hut.

Bid farewell to **Rifugio Chalet de l'Epée** (2370m) and take the clear path (AV2 and n.9) NNW contouring across slopes with flowering shrubs, bilberries and martagon lilies, not to mention marmots. A slow descent winds down to a farm track (**Praz-Londzet**, 2184m) where you go L (NW). Steady descent leads through pasture to a path in woodland due N.

This cuts down to the sports grounds and tarmac leading over a bridge to join the main road. Here it's R down to the main village of **Valgrisenche** (1664m, **1hr 50min**).

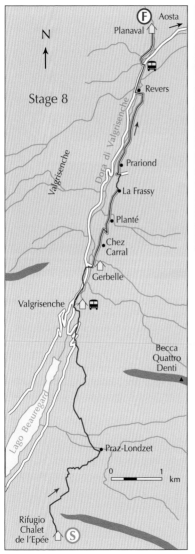

An old wooden crucifix in Valgrisenche

Valgrisenche offers tourist info (tel 339 8406922), bus, ATM, groceries. Accommodation at B&B Lo Souvenir (tel 345 9155087, https://www.bblo-souvenir.it/). A 10min uphill detour is dorm accommodation with meals at Le Vieux Quartier (tel 335 1213133, www.levieux-quartier.it).

At the intersection at the far end of the village, the AV2 veers L then R onto a path across meadows slightly above the road. About 1.2km on, follow the signs R to drop across the road and then the river to the hamlet of **Gerbelle** where you keep L (N) past B&B Maison Bovard (tel 346 0905728, www.maisonbovard.com). Walk

The hamlet of Revers in Valgrisenche

straight on via vegetable gardens through to **Chez Carral** (restaurant), then the cluster of houses at **La Frassy**. Soon you break off L to **Prariond** (1549m), which boasts
a curious monastery-like building, which is actually a historic stable and hayloft!

Without crossing the river, the AV2 takes a series of quiet lanes R (N)
to **Revers** (1530m) and a deliciously cool drinking fountain. The dramatic
gorge of the Dora di Valgrisenche is crossed here. At the main road go R
briefly to the fork L up to **Planaval** (1554m, **1hr 30min**), a modest farming
village set at the foot of sheer cliffs with a crashing waterfall. Here you will
find Hotel Paramount (accepts credit cards, tel 0165 97106, www.paramont
hotelristorante.com).

Note: If needed, it is possible to skip the long stages ahead and catch a bus
from Planaval down to the main Aosta valley then on to La Thuile to pick
up Stage 11.

STAGE 9

Planaval to Bivacco Cosimo Zappelli

Start	Planaval
Distance	10km
Total ascent	1400m
Total descent	700m
Grade	2–3
Time	5hr (opposite direction 4hr 30min)

Today the AV2 detours N to avoid the Ruitor glacier on a route that guarantees multiple rewards: beautiful wild valleys, very few other walkers and breathtaking views from the pass, Col de la Crosatie. Steep terrain with some exposure in descent follows the pass, so watch your step. The stage concludes in an isolated valley with only a handful of shepherds and livestock, not to mention comfortable Bivacco Cosimo Zappelli. The modern hut is unmanned, but water is available as are beds and blankets. At the time of writing there were no cooking facilities so you need your own food and a camping stove if you want a hot meal.

Note: Energy and weather permitting, if an overnight stay at the bivacco doesn't appeal or you're not equipped, press on to Rifugio Deffeyes – but be aware this means an extra 2hr 40min, bringing the day's total to 7hr 40min.

Leaving Planaval

From the hotel at **Planaval** (1554m) continue through the pretty farming village past the church and across the stream. Keep to the L fork towards the hamlet of **La Clusaz**, where the tarmac veers L below the houses. A batch of signposts soon point AV2 walkers to the path which begins its climb WNW through shady mixed woodland. With constant zigzags on the R bank of the

On the way to Baraques du Fond in the company of Testa del Ruitor

Torrent de Planaval and improving views over Valgrisenche, it reaches flower-covered mountainsides thick with crickets. The gradient eases temporarily as you enter an attractive valley with a meandering stream and marshes prickly with cotton grass and purple orchids. Ahead SW rises the Testa del Ruitor and its spreading glacier – quite a sight!

Slabs of glacially smoothed rock accompany you to a higher terrace and the picturesque abandoned huts of **Baraques du Fond** (2340m, **2hr 15min**). Here the AV2 parts ways with the route to Colle de Planaval and the glacier crossing, and turns R, initially W, in ascent to tiny **Lac du Fond** (2439m) nestling in a cup-shaped cirque.

At Col del la Crosatie

Now you embark on a perfectly graded ascent

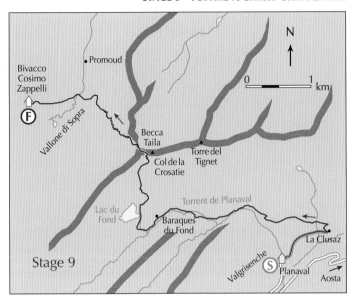

N, with steps occasionally cut into the rock face but no exposure to speak of. Enjoy the final views of Valgrisenche as you leave it behind for **Col de la Crosatie** (2838m, **1hr 30min**).

> Here the superbly magnificent line-up of the **Mont Blanc range** will take your breath away. Closer at hand Vallone di Sopra with Promoud is directly at your feet, while R of the pass is dark, dizzy rock point, Becca Taila, where the local goats play precarious hanging-on games.

A clear path plunges downhill NNW, with good solid steps aided by ropes traversing a massive stone-ridden slope. A couple of hundred metres lower down things become greener and alpenrose shrubs appear, in bloom if you are lucky. After a never-ending descent, around the 2100m mark, AV2 waymarks point you sharp L and quickly over a bridged stream. Up the other side you turn L (W) for a gentle climb to the peaceful location of **Bivacco Cosimo Zappelli** (2275m, **1hr 15min**). Property of Comune La Salle, it sleeps 10 with mattresses and blankets. Solar panels provide electricity. Tel 0165 861908.

STAGE 10

Bivacco Cosimo Zappelli to La Thuile

Start	Bivacco Cosimo Zappelli
Distance	14km
Total ascent	700m
Total descent	1500m
Grade	2
Time	5hr 40min (opposite direction 7hr)
Note	the August shuttle bus navetta from La Joux to La Thuile allows you to cut 45min off the day's load.

This beautifully varied and lengthy day sets out to traverse a panoramic col before enjoying a string of lakes that precede scenically positioned Rifugio Deffeyes. An excellent place to stay if you have time up your sleeve, this will allow a side trip towards the glacier, as well as a leisurely descent to La Thuile the following day. After the refuge comes a knee-weakening descent down a justifiably popular valley with a wealth of spectacular waterfalls. The stage concludes at the town of La Thuile, with a good range of facilities.

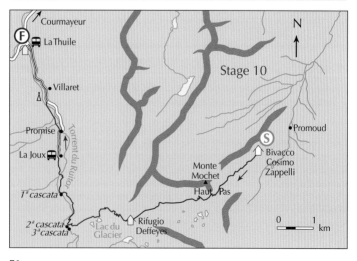

Leave **Bivacco Cosimo Zappelli** (2275m) uphill SW high above the meandering stream. As the wood gives out, stony slopes take over, the result of old rockfalls beneath Monte Mochet. A series of cirques follows and the gradient gets much steeper but the path is well waymarked and trouble-free. Steps fashioned out of rock slabs help you up to **Haut Pas** (2860m, **1hr 40min**) otherwise known as *Passo Alto*, below Testa di Paramont. Rewarding views range back over Valle d'Aosta to the icy, snow-covered sprawl of Monte Rosa. The E side of the pass is dotted with pretty turquoise tarns, the Lacs des Usselettes.

The AV2 winds easily downhill W. Rock-ridden flanks are succeeded by vast glacier-smoothed rocks and a cool stream in Comba des Usselettes. Picnic spots abound, although do remember that cotton grass means marshy terrain! Visible ahead is **Rifugio Deffeyes** (2500m, **1hr**).

RIFUGIO DEFFEYES

Rifugio Deffeyes and Grand Assalay

The refuge is marvellously located facing the lakes and glaciers on the 3846m Ruitor, which was first scaled in 1862 by English climbers Matthews and Bonney with Chamonix guide Michel Croz. It is well worth a stopover to explore the glacier at closer range on path n.16 that climbs SE towards Col de Planaval. The Grande Assaly is a distinct knife blade (SSW).

Sleeps 92, CAI, open June to Sept. Tel 0165 884239, www.rifugiodeffeyes.it.

The Ruitor glaciers admired from the descent path

A CAUTIONARY TALE

An age-old legend says that Ghiacciaio del Ruitor was once rich pasture. One day, the story goes, Christ was on earth to see what use man had made of the gifts bestowed on him. Disguised as a beggar he asked for a drink of milk, to which an ill-mannered shepherd retorted that he would rather pour his milk away than waste a drop on an old tramp – and rudely overturned a large pail.

His iniquity incurred the wrath of the Almighty. White streams gushed from the earth in a terrible wave of destruction, before freezing. The shepherd was trapped beneath the glacier, his rage causing the ice to creak and shift. Lakes and waterfalls were formed by his tears of frustration, icy cold like his heart and as bitter as his soul. No wonder the water here is undrinkable!

The glacier was much more extensive during the mini 19th century ice age, and its frontal barrier collapsed under the pressure of water and ice, causing terrible floods as far away as Villeneuve in Valle d'Aosta. As the ice sheet continues to retreat, it leaves hollows where lakes form, colouring the combas (long narrow glacial valleys) with their turquoise hues.

The long descent now commences on a pleasant mule track NW into a vast valley trough of accumulated silt and the stunning **Lac du Glacier** (2140m), backed by Col Lex Blanche at the head of Vallon de la Belle Combe. The path heads W up and down across rocks and into the welcome shade of flowered woods. It draws closer to the stream that descends from the Ruitor glacier and there are soon marked detours off L to viewpoints for the powerful waterfalls, marked **3a cascata** then **2a cascata** (third and second waterfall).

As the water thunders down the **rock channel**, sprays of cool suspended mist are whipped over unsuspecting visitors by the lightest breeze. Daring shrubs cling to overhangs, benefitting from the natural irrigation system.

The main path continues NW valleywards passing a deep-cut rock channel to an excellent viewpoint for the **1a cascata** (first waterfall). Not long afterwards you cross Torrent du Ruitor to **La Joux** (1603m, **2hr 15min**) (refreshments, car park and free August shuttle bus to La Thuile).

Turn R along the tarmac. Immediately after a rise comes a sequence of signed shortcuts that keep you away from the traffic. After touching on the road at **Promise** (1515m) you keep L of the stream and take a forestry track past former Soggiorno Firenze.

Not far from Camping Rutor (tel 333 1372961, http://campingrutor.altervista. org) tarmac is joined for the last leg through Villaret and down to the main road at **La Thuile** (1447m, **45min**).

LA THUILE

A popular winter resort, La Thuile needs little introduction to British skiers. Its name derives from either 'tegula' stone roofing slabs, or Tullius Cicero, Caesar's lieutenant during the wars against the Gauls (54–52BC).

La Thuile offers year-round buses to Courmayeur and Aosta, groceries, bakery, ATM. The accommodation range includes Hotel Coeur du Village (tel 0165 04340, awww.hotelcoeurduvillage.com).

STAGE 11
La Thuile to Rifugio Elisabetta Soldini

Start	La Thuile
Distance	18km
Total ascent	1200m
Total descent	490m
Grade	2
Time	4hr 45min (opposite direction 4hr)

This second-last stage is the AV2's last day of relative solitude. It is straightforward if a little monotonous initially during the lengthy climb, however the abundance of unusual wildflowers (even orchids) provides excellent distraction and the spectacular pass is ample compensation. After days and days of gradual approach with teasing glimpses, today the full glory of the Mont Blanc line-up is revealed (out with the PeakFinder app). Clear weather is naturally preferable. The ensuing drop concludes at comfortable Rifugio Elisabetta Soldini, usually crowded with walkers on the Tour of Mont Blanc, so book well ahead in high season. An alternative is to continue 45min downhill to Cabane du Combal (see Stage 12).

On the main road at **La Thuile** (1447m) walk downhill about 150m to a clutch of yellow signposts pointing you L across the river past Hotel Miramonti and onto a paved track. In ascent mostly SW, it cuts the bends of the road that ascends to the Piccolo San Bernardo pass. About half an hour on, near **Pont Serrand** (1602m), AV2 walkers are directed sharp R (W) onto a narrow farm road (also n.11), in the company of noisy crickets on sun-beaten pasture. It leads past dairy farms and eatery, Ristoro Chez Le Lapin, before terminating at **Porassey** (1900m). A lane continues N through the narrow entrance of a long, treeless but thickly flow-ered pasture valley, Vallone di Chavannes. The bare slopes are the perfect hunting grounds for birds of prey. Climbing gradually NNW, the route offers stunning views back to the Ruitor. Make sure you keep R at the 2244m fork for the slog up past the **Chavannes d'en haut** (2424m) farm huts. The final stretch means a traverse due W to the day's highlight **Col des Chavannes** (2603m, **3hr 45min**).

Breathtaking views from Col des Chavannes

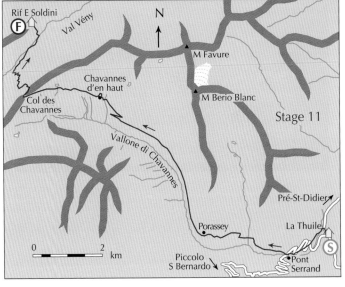

Rif E Soldini

Val Vény

F

N

M Favure

Chavannes
d'en haut

M Berio Blanc

Col des
Chavannes

Stage 11

Vallone di Chavannes

Pré-St-Didier

Porassey

La Thuile

0   2 km

S

Piccolo
S Bernardo

Pont
Serrand

You probably won't be vaguely interested in the chamois on the neighbouring cols or the playful marmots, outdone by the dazzling mountains ahead over Val Vény with glaciers spilling every which way. Anything else is instantly forgotten as awe-inspiring **Mont Blanc** appears abruptly right in front of you.

Once you've got your breath back and exhausted all the photo opportunities, drop N still on the n.11, zigzagging easily if pretty steeply down grassy slopes dotted with pretty alpine thrift. The broad base of Vallon de la Lex Blanche, site of an ancient Roman road, is quickly gained beneath the sheer limestone walls of the remarkable Pyramides Calcaires. A delightful stroll R (NE) concludes with the brief climb past an old military hut and marmot burrows close to the immense icefall of the Ghiacciaio de la Lex Blanche, to family-run **Rifugio Elisabetta Soldini** (2197m, **1hr**).

RIFUGIO ELISABETTA SOLDINI

Rifugio Elisabetta at the foot of the awesome Lex Blanche glacier

At this bustling refuge you'll encounter walkers from all over the world on the Tour of Mont Blanc (TMB). The hot water comes thanks to the turbine that harnesses energy from the glacier.

Sleeps 80, CAI, open early June to early Oct. Booking well in advance recommended. Tel 0165 844080, www.rifugioelisabetta.com.

STAGE 12

Rifugio Elisabetta Soldini to Courmayeur

Start	Rifugio Elisabetta Soldini
Distance	15km
Total ascent	500m
Total descent	1500m
Grade	2
Time	4hr 45min (opposite direction 5hr)

This final stage is in common with the TMB. It is a fitting conclusion to the AV2 and is problem-free. The central part is a wonderful traverse with stunning views towards the Mont Blanc range so allow lots of extra time for photographic stops. The final descent is (understandably) less spectacular due to the bulldozed slopes for winter skiing. However, it can always be shortened: by jeep taxi from Maison Vieille, or by a ride on lifts via Plan Chécrouit to Courmayeur, saving 1hr 30min and 700m descent. On the other hand, walkers reluctant to conclude this marvellous trek can postpone their return to civilisation and stay another night in one of the comfortable chalets encountered en route. Those intending to camp will need to take the Val Vény alternative. The unlucky few caught up in bad weather at Rifugio Elisabetta Soldini are advised either to wait it out or bail out via the same valley route to Courmayeur – see below.

Leave **Rifugio Elisabetta Soldini** (2197m) on the wide track NE to the valley floor where marshy streams make for lovely reflections and cloudy glacier melt merges with clear water. Ahead a curious, seemingly man-made ridge attempts to bar the valley. It is the line of lateral moraine shoved aside by the huge Miage glacier. Down at **Lago Combal** (2000m, **45min**), continue to the far end where a brief detour L over the torrent leads to café-resto-refuge Cabane du Combal (sleeps 23, accepts credit cards, open June–Sept, tel 0165 1756421 or 339 6938817, www. cabaneducombal.com).

A fascinating 30min detour leads to the constantly changing shape of murky, milky-grey Lago Miage, imprisoned by the encroaching moraine and ice bulldozer that topples trees in its path. Walkers intending to stay low and take the Val Vény route for Courmayeur part ways with the official AV2 route here.

Val Vény exit route to Courmayeur (1hr 15min + bus or 3hr)

Walk down the road NE, by all means following the path alternatives. **La Visaille** (1659m, **1hr 15min**) has a cafè-restaurant, as well as July–Aug bus to Courmayeur. The path to fascinating Giardino di Miage starts here, a weird pocket garden of larch trees trapped between the advancing arms of the ice mass.

For the remaining 7km, in the absence of a bus, continue on road and paths past campsites such as Camping Aiguille Noire (tel 347 5477941, www. aiguillenoire.com), with great views over to the Brenva glacier and of course Mont Blanc. A final landmark is the chapel of **Notre Dame de la Guérison**, an impassable barrier for the multitude of devils and witches banished to the high icy realms of Val Vény. Take care on the road as you round the corner of the main floor of Valle d'Aosta. Ignore the junction L across to **La Saxe**, and walk on for Entrelevie. It's then a short stroll over the Dora Baltea river to **Courmayeur** (1223m, **1hr 45min**).

Main route continued

Staying with the AV2/TMB, at the end of **Lago Combal**, you break off abruptly R (E) shortly before a bridge. A steady climb SSE leads past an abandoned summer farm and over pasture to the silent Alpe superiore de l'Arpe Vieille (2302m).

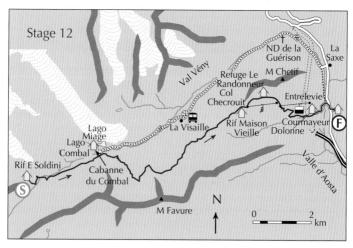

Lago Combal gives gorgeous reflections

A swing to detour a spur of Monte Favure brings you to today's highest point (2400m). It goes without saying that every step taken is rewarded with increasingly awesome views of the Miage glacier and Mont Blanc, along with amazing aiguilles (rock needles). Contouring NE you walk through flowered pasture basins and soon begin to encounter winter ski lifts and pistes. Across the valley is the sprawl of the mighty Brenva glacier at the rear of the Aiguille Noire de Peuterey. Gentle descent through light woodland leads to the broad saddle of **Col Checrouit** (1956m, **2hr 15min**) close to the rock triangle Mont Chetif. An overnight stay or al fresco lunch can be enjoyed at **Rifugio Maison Vieille** (1956m) (sleeps 60, accepts credit cards, open mid June to Sept. Jeep taxi and luggage service to Courmayeur. Tel 337 230979 or 328 0584157, www.maisonvieille.com.) Close by is a mid-summer chair lift that connects to the Plan Chécrouit cable-car to Courmayeur.

Keep NE down a broad dirt track to the refuge-resto **Le Randonneur** (1894m) (sleeps 25, accepts credit cards, open early June to early Sept, tel 349 5368898 or 320 4303540, www.randonneurmb.com).

Trekkers enjoy a well-earned rest at Maison Vieille

Now you're pointed S on paths and tracks beneath lifts and across ski pistes to Plan Chécrouit (1701m, **30min**), with an upmarket hotel and the Courmayeur *funivia* (cable-car).

The AV2/TMB keeps L down a narrow path in decisive descent E cutting through conifer woods. At a dirt road you veer L for the last leg downhill – watch your step here in the wet. You finally enter **Dolonne** (1210m, **1hr**), a charming village with a photogenic washing trough and hotels such as Hotel Ottoz (tel 0165 846681, www.hotelottoz.net).

Clear signs point walkers through the maze of narrow streets and out to the main road. The Dora Baltea river is crossed and a short way uphill is the bus station and tourist office of cosmopolitan **Courmayeur** (1223m, **15min**).

Courmayeur offers a wide choice of accommodation such as Pensione Venezia (tel 0165 842461, pensionevenezia@gmail.com) and Edelweiss (tel 0165 841590, www.albergoedelweiss.it). It also has a tourist office, shops galore, daily coaches to Aosta (trains) and beyond, or through to Chamonix in France.

An exciting follow-up treat to the Valle d'Aosta's Alta Via 2 is a trip over the awe-inspiring **Mont Blanc massif** by a series of spectacular cable-cars. A local bus will drop you at La Palud on the outskirts of Courmayeur, from where you can make the 1hr 45min adventure all the way over to Chamonix in France (www.montebianco.com). Buses run back through the Mont Blanc tunnel, referred to as the 'Traforo di Monte Bianco' in Italian.

APPENDIX A

Italian–English glossary

Italian	English
acqua (non) potabile	water (not) suitable for drinking
affittacamere	B&B
agibile (inagibile)	in good (bad) condition, referring to a hut or route
aiuto!	help!
Albergo	hotel
alpage, alpe	summer pasture area and/or hut
alta via	long distance high level route
alto	high
altopiano, altipiano	high altitude plateau
autostazione	bus station
balma	old shepherds' dwellings with dry-stone walls
becca, cima, punta, testa	mountain peak, summit
bivacco	unmanned bivouac hut
bocca, bocchetta, col, colle, finestra, fenêtre, passo	mountain pass
borgata, frazione, hameau	hamlet
cabinovia	gondola lift
caduta sassi	falling rocks
camere libere	rooms available
capanna, casolare, casotto	hut
cascata	waterfall
cengia	ledge
comba, combe	long narrow valley
costa	flank, slope
cresta	crest, ridge
dessot/dessus	lower/upper
diga	dam
est/orientale	east/eastern
facile	easy
finestra, fenêtre	literally 'window', col, pass
fiume	river
funivia	cable-car

Italian	English
ghiacciaio	glacier
grangia	stone shepherd's hut, used seasonally
lac (lacs), lago (laghi)	lake (lakes)
mayen	medium-altitude farm that can be utilised early (such as May, hence the name) to provide livestock with fresh grass
montagna	high altitude summer farm in Valle d'Aosta
muanda	high altitude summer farm in Piemonte
nord/settentrionale	north/northern
ovest/occidentale	west/western
palestra di roccia	rock-climbing area
passeggiata	promenade
pedonale	for pedestrians
percorso	route
pericolo/pericoloso	danger/dangerous
piano	plain, plateau when a noun (slowly or quietly, when an adverb)
ponte	bridge
prato	meadow
ricovero invernale	winter quarters adjoining a refuge
rifugio	mountain hut, usually manned
rio, torrente	mountain stream
san, santo, santa	saint
seggiovia	chair lift
sentiero	path
soccorso alpino	mountain rescue
sorgente	spring (water)
stazione ferroviaria	railway station
sud/meridionale	south/southern
telecabina	gondola car
tornante	hairpin bend
torre	tower
traforo	road tunnel
val, valle, vallon, vallone	valley

APPENDIX B
Useful contacts

The visitor centres of the Parco Nazionale del Gran Paradiso handy for AV2 walkers are at Cogne, Rhêmes-Notre-Dame (Chavaney), not to mention the fascinating Alpine Botanical Garden at Valnontey. See www.pngp.it.

Useful tourist information offices, referred to as Ufficio Turistico or Pro Loco, are located at:

Aosta
Tel 0165 236627
www.lovevda.it

Champorcher
Tel 0125 37134
www.valledichamporcher.it

Cogne
Tel 0165 74040
www.cogneturismo.it

Courmayeur
Tel 0165 842060
www.courmayeurmontblanc.it

Dégioz
Tel 0165 905816

La Thuile
Tel 0165 884179
www.lathuile.it

Pont, Valsavarenche
Tel 0165 95304 (summer)

Rhêmes-Notre-Dame
Tel 0165 936114
www.rhemesturismo.it

Valgrisenche
Tel 339 8406922
www.prolocovalgrisenche.com

NOTES

DOWNLOAD THE GPX FILES

All the routes in this guide are available for download from:

www.cicerone.co.uk/1184/GPX

as standard format GPX files. You should be able to load them into most online GPX systems and mobile devices, whether GPS or smartphone. You may need to convert the file into your preferred format using a conversion programme such as gpsvisualizer.com or one of the many other such websites and programmes.

When you follow this link, you will be asked for your email address and where you purchased the guidebook, and have the option to subscribe to the Cicerone e-newsletter.

LISTING OF CICERONE GUIDES

BRITISH ISLES CHALLENGES, COLLECTIONS AND ACTIVITIES
Great Walks on the England Coast Path
Map and Compass
The Big Rounds
The Book of the Bivvy
The Book of the Bothy
The Mountains of England and Wales:
   Vol 1 Wales
   Vol 2 England
The National Trails
Walking the End to End Trail

SHORT WALKS SERIES
Short Walks Hadrian's Wall
Short Walks in the Lake District: Keswick, Borrowdale and Buttermere
Short Walks in the Lake District: Windermere Ambleside and Grasmere
Short Walks in the Lake District: Coniston and Langdale
Short Walks in Arnside and Silverdale
Short Walks in Nidderdale
Short Walks in Northumberland: Wooler, Rothbury, Alnwick and the coast
Short Walks on the Malvern Hills
Short Walks in Cornwall: Falmouth and the Lizard
Short Walks in Cornwall: Land's End and Penzance
Short Walks in the South Downs: Brighton, Eastbourne and Arundel
Short Walks in the Surrey Hills
Short Walks Winchester
Short Walks in Pembrokeshire: Tenby and the south
Short Walks on the Isle of Mull
Short Walks on the Orkney Islands

SCOTLAND
Ben Nevis and Glen Coe
Cycling in the Hebrides
Cycling the North Coast 500
Great Mountain Days in Scotland
Mountain Biking in Southern and Central Scotland
Mountain Biking in West and North West Scotland
Not the West Highland Way Scotland
Scotland's Best Small Mountains
Scotland's Mountain Ridges
Scottish Wild Country Backpacking
Short Walks in Dumfries and Galloway
Skye's Cuillin Ridge Traverse
The Borders Abbeys Way
The Great Glen Way

The Great Glen Way Map Booklet
The Hebridean Way
The Hebrides
The Isle of Mull
The Isle of Skye
The Skye Trail
The Southern Upland Way
The West Highland Way
West Highland Way Map Booklet
Walking Ben Lawers, Rannoch and Atholl
Walking in the Cairngorms
Walking in the Pentland Hills
Walking in the Scottish Borders
Walking in the Southern Uplands
Walking in Torridon, Fisherfield, Fannichs and An Teallach
Walking Loch Lomond and the Trossachs
Walking on Arran
Walking on Harris and Lewis
Walking on Jura, Islay and Colonsay
Walking on Rum and the Small Isles
Walking on the Orkney and Shetland Isles
Walking on Uist and Barra
Walking the Cape Wrath Trail
Walking the Corbetts
   Vol 1 South of the Great Glen
   Vol 2 North of the Great Glen
Walking the Galloway Hills
Walking the John o' Groats Trail
Walking the Munros
   Vol 1 — Southern, Central and Western Highlands
   Vol 2 — Northern Highlands and the Cairngorms
Winter Climbs in the Cairngorms
Winter Climbs: Ben Nevis and Glen Coe

NORTHERN ENGLAND ROUTES
Cycling the Reivers Route
Cycling the Way of the Roses
Hadrian's Cycleway
Hadrian's Wall Path
Hadrian's Wall Path Map Booklet
Pennine Way Map Booklet
The Coast to Coast Cycle Route
The Coast to Coast Walk
The Coast to Coast Map Booklet
The Pennine Way
Walking the Dales Way
The Dales Way Map Booklet

LAKE DISTRICT
Bikepacking in the Lake District
Cycling in the Lake District
Great Mountain Days in the Lake District
Joss Naylor's Lakes, Meres and Waters of the Lake District

Lake District Winter Climbs
Lake District:
   High Level and Fell Walks
   Low Level and Lake Walks
Mountain Biking in the Lake District
Outdoor Adventures with Children — Lake District
Scrambles in the Lake District —
   North
   South
Trail and Fell Running in the Lake District
Walking The Cumbria Way
Walking the Lake District Fells —
   Borrowdale
   Buttermere
   Coniston
   Keswick
   Langdale
   Mardale and the Far East
   Patterdale
   Wasdale
Walking the Tour of the Lake District

NORTH—WEST ENGLAND AND THE ISLE OF MAN
Cycling the Pennine Bridleway
Isle of Man Coastal Path
The Lancashire Cycleway
The Lune Valley and Howgills
Walking in Cumbria's Eden Valley
Walking in Lancashire
Walking in the Forest of Bowland and Pendle
Walking on the Isle of Man
Walking on the West Pennine Moors
Walking the Ribble Way
Walks in Silverdale and Arnside

NORTH—EAST ENGLAND, YORKSHIRE DALES AND PENNINES
Cycling in the Yorkshire Dales
Great Mountain Days in the Pennines
Mountain Biking in the Yorkshire Dales
The Cleveland Way and the Yorkshire Wolds Way
The Cleveland Way Map Booklet
The North York Moors
Trail and Fell Running in the Yorkshire Dales
Walking in County Durham
Walking in Northumberland
Walking in the North Pennines
Walking in the Yorkshire Dales:
   North and East
   South and West
Walking St Cuthbert's Way
Walking St Oswald's Way and Northumberland Coast Path

For full information on all our
guides, books and eBooks,
visit our website:
www.cicerone.co.uk

CICERONE

Trust Cicerone to guide your next adventure,
wherever it may be around the world...

Discover guides for hiking, mountain walking, backpacking,
trekking, trail running, cycling and mountain biking, ski touring,
climbing and scrambling in Britain, Europe and worldwide.

Connect with Cicerone online and find inspiration.

- buy books and ebooks
- articles, advice and trip reports
- GPX files and updates
- regular newsletter

cicerone.co.uk